Zaner-Bloser Handwriting

With a simplified alphabet

Author

Clinton S. Hackney

Contributing Authors

Pamela J. Farris
Janice T. Jones
Linda Leonard Lamme

Zaner-Bloser, Inc., P.O. Box 16764, Columbus, Ohio 43216-6764   1-800-421-3018

Copyright © 1999 Zaner-Bloser, Inc.   ISBN 0-88085-957-1

Developed by Kirchoff/Wohlberg, Inc., in cooperation with Zaner-Bloser Publishers

Printed in the United States of America

98 99 00 01 02 WC 5 4 3 2 1

You already know handwriting is important.
Now take a look at...

NEW SIMPLIFIED

Zaner-Bloser Handwriting

Easier to read!   Easier to write!   Easier to teach!

I see Zaner-Bloser's
alphabet in the books I read.

Zaner-Bloser's new
program is easy to teach.

I like Zaner-Bloser because
it's so easy to write.

Did You Know...

Annually, the U.S. Postal Service receives 38 million illegibly addressed letters, costing American taxpayers $4 million each year.

–American Demographics, Dec. 1992

Did You Know...

Hundreds of thousands of tax returns are delayed every year because figures, notes, and signatures are illegible.

–Better Handwriting in 30 Days, 1989

Did You Know...

Poor handwriting costs American business $200 million annually.

–American Demographics, Dec. 1992

iii

Zaner-Bloser's CONTINUOUS-STROKE manuscript alphabet

Aa Bb Cc Dd Ee Ff Gg
Oo Pp Qq Rr Ss Tt

Easier to Read

Our vertical manuscript alphabet is like the alphabet kids see every day inside and outside of the classroom. They see it in their school books, in important environmental print like road signs, and in books and cartoons they read for fun.

"[Slanted] manuscript is not only harder to learn than traditional [vertical] print, but it creates substantially more letter recognition errors and causes more letter confusion than does the traditional style."

–Debby Kuhl and Peter Dewitz in a paper presented at the 1994 meeting of the American Educational Research Association

Please, my friends, a moment of silence, as the flying Zucchinis attempt a twisting triple somersault.

CALIFORNIA LIN 216

STOP

Vertical manuscript is the alphabet we see every day.

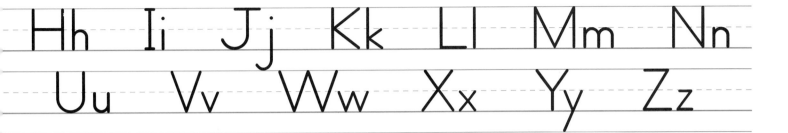
Hh Ii Jj Kk Ll Mm Nn
Uu Vv Ww Xx Yy Zz

Easier to Write

Our vertical manuscript alphabet is written with continuous strokes—fewer pencil lifts—so there's a greater sense of flow in writing. And kids can write every letter once they learn four simple strokes that even kindergartners can manage.

Four simple strokes: circle, horizontal line, vertical line, slanted line

"The writing hand has to change direction more often when writing the [slanted] alphabet, do more retracing of lines, and make more strokes that occur later in children's development."

–Steve Graham in *Focus on Exceptional Children*, 1992

Many kids can already write their names when they start school (vertical manuscript).

Kirk

Why should they have to relearn them in another form (slanted manuscript)? With Zaner-Bloser, they don't have to.

Kirk

Easier to Teach

Our vertical manuscript alphabet is easy to teach because there's no reteaching involved. Children are already familiar with our letterforms—they've seen them in their environment and they've learned them at home.

"Before starting school, many children learn how to write traditional [vertical] manuscript letters from their parents or preschool teachers. Learning a special alphabet such as [slanted] means that these children will have to relearn many of the letters they can already write."

–Steve Graham in *Focus on Exceptional Children*, 1992

Zaner-Bloser's NEW SIMPLIFIED cursive alphabet

Aa Bb Cc Dd Ee Ff Gg

Nn Oo Pp Qq Rr Ss

Simplified letterforms...
Easier to read and write

old letterform

Letterforms are simplified so they're easier to write and easier to identify in writing. The new simplified **Q** now looks like a **Q** instead of a number 2.

old letterform

Our simplified letterforms use the headline, midline, and baseline as a guide for where letters start and stop. The new simplified **d** touches the headline instead of stopping halfway.

old letterform

No more "cane stems!" Our new simplified letterforms begin with a small curve instead of fancy loops that can be difficult for students to write.

Hh Ii Jj Kk Ll Mm
Tt Uu Vv Ww Xx Yy Zz

Simplified letterforms...
Easier to teach

When handwriting is easy for students to write, instruction time is cut way back! That's the teaching advantage with Zaner-Bloser Handwriting. Our cursive letter-forms are simplified so instead of spending a lot of time teaching fancy loops that give kids trouble, teachers give instruction for simple, basic handwriting that students can use for the rest of their lives.

And remember, with Zaner-Bloser Handwriting, students learn to write manuscript with continuous strokes. That means that when it's time for those students to begin writing cursive, the transition comes naturally because they already know the flow of contin-uous strokes.

These simple letters are so much easier to teach!

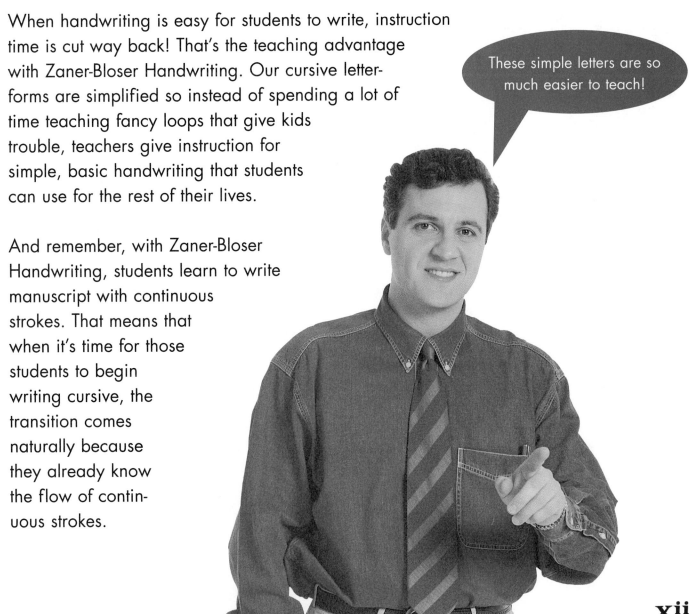

The Student Edition...set up for student success

Students trace models first before writing on their own.

A clear connection is made between the manuscript and cursive forms of each letter.

Writing practice is done directly beneath a model that is easy for both right- and left-handers to see.

Students write letters first, then practice joinings, and finally write complete words and sentences.

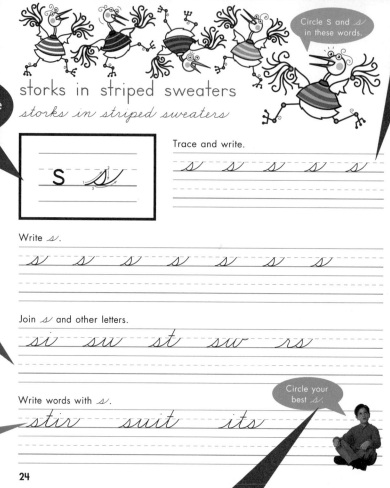

Circle S and *s* in these words.

storks in striped sweaters
storks in striped sweaters

S *s*

Trace and write.
s s s s s

Write *s*.
s s s s s s s

Join *s* and other letters.
si su st sw rs

Write words with *s*.
stir suit its

Circle your best *s*.

24

Grade 3 Student Edition

Students evaluate their own handwriting on every page.

Language arts connections are easy with activities like this one. Here, students learn what idioms are and translate some well-known idioms as they practice their handwriting.

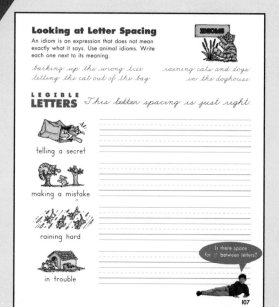

Looking at Letter Spacing

An idiom is an expression that does not mean exactly what it says. Use animal idioms. Write each one next to its meaning.

barking up the wrong tree
telling the cat out of the bag

raining cats and dogs
in the doghouse

LEGIBLE LETTERS *This letter spacing is just right.*

telling a secret

making a mistake

raining hard

in trouble

Is there space for it between letters?

107

Grade 3 Student Edition

Correct letter models are easy for all students to see.

Letters and joinings are practiced in each review.

Students evaluate their own handwriting.

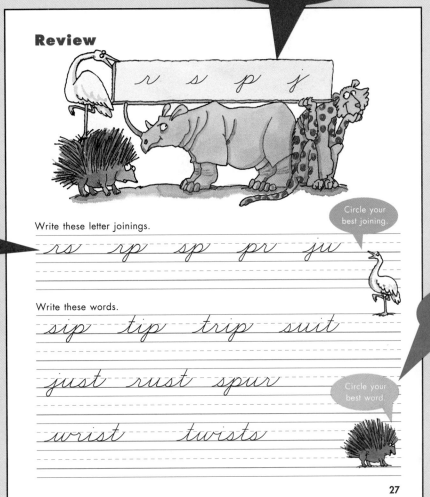

Review
r s p j
Write these letter joinings.
rs rp sp pr ju
Circle your best joining.
Write these words.
sip tip trip suit
just rust spur
wrist twists
Circle your best word.
27

Grade 3 Student Edition

Students learn to appreciate diverse cultures through activities like this one, in which they write "cap" and "ball" in several different languages.

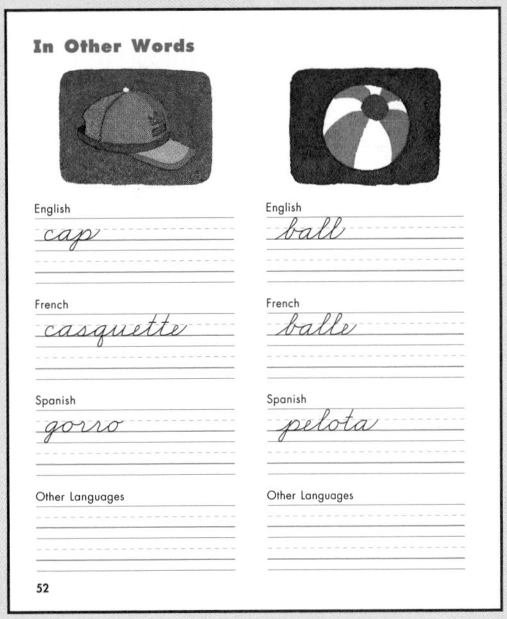

In Other Words
English
cap
English
ball
French
casquette
French
balle
Spanish
gorro
Spanish
pelota
Other Languages
Other Languages
52

Grade 3 Student Edition

The Teacher Edition...streamlined instruction

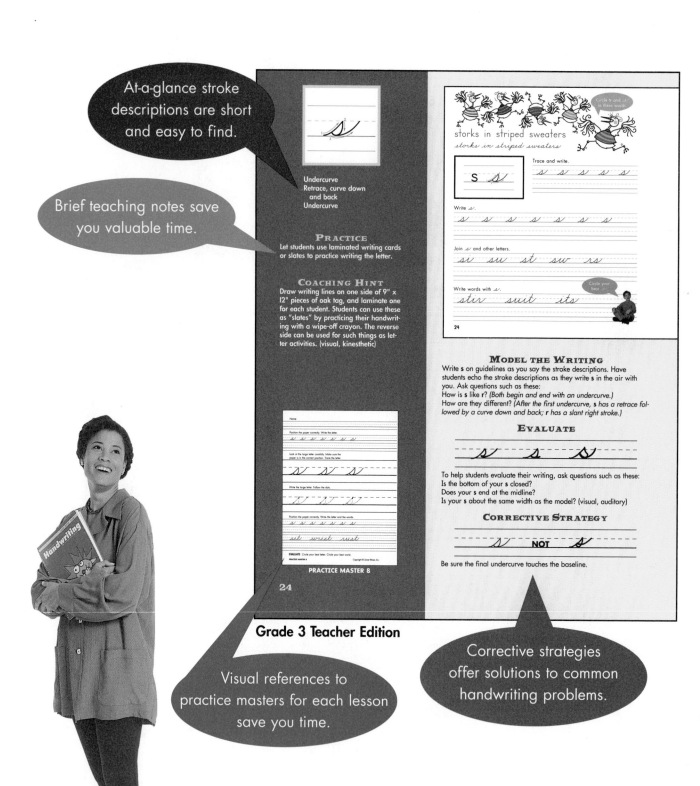

At-a-glance stroke descriptions are short and easy to find.

Brief teaching notes save you valuable time.

Visual references to practice masters for each lesson save you time.

Corrective strategies offer solutions to common handwriting problems.

Grade 3 Teacher Edition

Undercurve
Retrace, curve down and back
Undercurve

PRACTICE
Let students use laminated writing cards or slates to practice writing the letter.

COACHING HINT
Draw writing lines on one side of 9" x 12" pieces of oak tag, and laminate one for each student. Students can use these as "slates" by practicing their handwriting with a wipe-off crayon. The reverse side can be used for such things as letter activities. (visual, kinesthetic)

PRACTICE MASTER 8

24

storks in striped sweaters

Trace and write.

Write s.

Join s and other letters.

Write words with s.
stir   suit   its

24

MODEL THE WRITING
Write s on guidelines as you say the stroke descriptions. Have students echo the stroke descriptions as they write s in the air with you. Ask questions such as these:
How is s like r? (Both begin and end with an undercurve.)
How are they different? (After the first undercurve, s has a retrace followed by a curve down and back; r has a slant right stroke.)

EVALUATE
To help students evaluate their writing, ask questions such as these:
Is the bottom of your s closed?
Does your s end at the midline?
Is your s about the same width as the model? (visual, auditory)

CORRECTIVE STRATEGY

NOT

Be sure the final undercurve touches the baseline.

The student page is close to the instruction for that page.

Review

Write these letter joinings.

rs rp sp pr ju

Write these words.

sip tip trip suit

just rust spur

wrist twists

27

EVALUATE

To help students evaluate their writing, ask questions such as these:
Are your joinings formed correctly?
Do **r**, **s**, **p**, and **j** touch the midline?
Do the descenders in **p** and **j** fill the descender space? (visual, auditory)

REFOCUS

Review the letters **r, s, p,** and **j** by asking questions such as these:
How do all the letters begin? *(with an undercurve)*
Which of these letters ends differently? *(The j ends with an overcurve.)*
Which letters have a descender? *(p, j)*
Review the joining techniques by writing the following combinations on the chalkboard. Say the strokes as you write them.

ji   tr   uw   sp
st   wi   ju   wr

Have students write each combination three times on paper. Suggest they underline their best joining.

COACHING HINT:
LEFT-HANDED
WRITERS
You might want to group left-handed students together for handwriting lessons.

WRITE AWAY

Ask students to imagine that a porcupine could talk. Have them write a question they would like to ask a porcupine. Participate by asking a question you would like to ask a porcupine.

27

HANDWRITING AND THE WRITING PROCESS

Activities are suggested throughout the Teacher Edition that emphasize the importance of using legible handwriting in all the steps of the writing process.

MAINTAINING MANUSCRIPT

These activities emphasize the need for maintaining good manuscript in many situations throughout life, such as writing envelopes, job applications, test forms, and bank forms.

Coaching Hints offer insight and additional information.

Language arts connections reinforce writing and other skills.

Grade 3 Teacher Edition

Grade 3 Practice Masters

An accompanying book of practice masters offers additional practice for every letter and skill students learn. It also includes resources to make teaching easier—certificates, an evaluation record, letters to send home to keep parents and guardians involved, and Spanish activities.

Evaluation and Assessment...
consistent guidance throughout the year

Student self-evaluation...

In every lesson. Students evaluate their own handwriting and circle their best work.

In every review. Fifteen times during the year, students review the letterforms and joinings they've learned and again evaluate their handwriting.

Through the keys to legibility. Students learn about the keys to legibility and apply what they've learned in special handwriting activities. Every one of these lessons places an emphasis on student self-evaluation.

Teacher assessment...

In every lesson and review. As students evaluate their own writing, teachers can assess their letterforms, as well as their comprehension of good handwriting. Corrective Strategies for each lesson offer teachers helpful hints for common handwriting problems.

Through personal writing activities. Students' personal writing offers lots of opportunity for informal assessment of handwriting, language arts, and other areas.

The Keys to Legibility

These four Keys to Legibility are taught and reviewed throughout the program.
They remind students that their goal should be legible handwriting.

Size

Consistently sized letters are easy to read. Students learn to use midlines and headlines to guide the size of their letters.

Slant

Letters with a consistent slant are easy to read. Students learn how to position their papers and hold their pencils so consistent slant comes with ease.

Shape

Four simple strokes—undercurve, downcurve, overcurve, and slant—make it easy for students to write letters with consistent and proper shape.

Spacing

Correct spacing between letters and words makes handwriting easy to read. Practical hints show students how to determine correct spacing.

Looking at Word Spacing

Say each tongue twister three times as fast as you can. Then write it.

LEGIBLE LETTERS *This word spacing is just right.*

Little lemmings like lots of lemons.

Little lemmings like lots of lemons.

Monkeys mix millions of muffins.

Monkeys mix millions of muffins.

Dalmatian digs dozens of daylilies.

Dalmatian digs dozens of daylilies.

Is there space for \ between words?

On Your Own Write a tongue twister you know.

Peter Piper picked a peck of pickled peppers.

108

Completed Grade 3 Student Edition

Personal writing activities allow the teacher to informally assess handwriting and language skills.

jumping
jumping
brought
brought
another
another
xylophone
xylophone
unable   trick
unable   trick

Circle your best joining in each word.

Put an **x** under a joining that could be better.

57

Students circle their best handwriting and also show where they need more work.

A huge collection of supplementary materials... makes handwriting even easier to teach!

A **Evaluation Guides** *grades 1–6*

B **Poster/Wall Chart Super Pak**
grades K–6, includes Handwriting Positions
Wall Chart, Keys to Legibility Wall Chart,
Alphabet Wall Chart, Simplified Stroke
Descriptions, and a Portfolio Assessment Guide

C **Story Journals** *grades K–4*

D **Manuscript/Cursive Card Set** *grades 1–6*

E **Sentence Strips** *grades K–6*

F **Writing Journals** *grades 1–6*

G **My ABC Journal** *grades K–1*

H **Pignic Alphabet Book** *grades K–2*

I **From Anne to Zach Alphabet Book** *grades K–2*

J **Letter Cards** *grades K–2*

K **Manuscript/Cursive Fonts**

L **Manuscript Kin-Tac Cards** *grades K–2*

For more information about these materials, call 1-800-421-3018.

M **Make-Your-Own Big Book** *grades K–2*

N **Parent Brochures** *for manuscript/cursive*

O **Book of Transparencies** *grades 1–6*

P **Read, Write, and Color Alphabet Mat**
grades K–2

Q **Dry Erase Write-On Cards** *grades K–2*

R **Parent/Student Worksheets** *grades 2–6*

S **Peek Thrus** *grades 1–4*

T **Illustrated Alphabet Strips** *grades K–4*

U **Desk Strips** *grades 1–6*

V **Practice Masters** *grades K–6*

W **Alphabet Wall Strips** *grades K–6*

X **Fun With Handwriting** *grades K–8*

Y **Write-On, Wipe-Off Magnetic Board
With Letters** *grades K–2*

Z **Post Office Kit** *grades K–4*

Vertical vs. *Slanted Manuscript*

What the research shows

Using a slanted alphabet has been a trend in handwriting instruction. It's actually not a new development—the first slanted alphabet was created in 1968. A sort of bridge between manuscript and cursive, this slanted alphabet used unconnected letterforms like the traditional vertical manuscript, but its letterforms were slanted like cursive.

It seemed like a good idea. This alphabet was to be easier to write than cursive, yet similar enough to cursive that children wouldn't learn two *completely* different alphabets. But after several years of use in some schools, research has uncovered some unfortunate findings.

Slanted manuscript can be difficult to write

Slanted manuscript was created to be similar to cursive, so it uses more complicated strokes such as small curves, and these strokes can be difficult for young children.

Vertical manuscript, on the other hand, is consistent with the development of young children. Each of its letters is formed with simple strokes—straight lines, circles, and slanted lines. One researcher found that the strokes used in vertical manuscript are the same as the shapes children use in their drawings (Farris, 1993). Because children are familiar with these shapes, they can identify and form the strokes with little difficulty.

Slanted manuscript can create problems with legibility

Legibility is an important goal in handwriting. Obviously, content should not be sacrificed for legibility, but what is handwriting if it cannot be read?

Educational researchers have tested the legibility of slanted manuscript and found that children writing vertical manuscript "performed significantly better" than those writing slanted manuscript. The writers of the slanted alphabet tended to make more misshapen letterforms, tended to extend their strokes above and below the guidelines, and had a difficult time keeping their letterforms consistent in size (Graham, 1992).

On the other hand, the vertical manuscript style of print has a lot of support in the area of research. Advertisers have known for years that italic type has a lower readability rate than vertical "roman" type. Research shows that in 30 minute readings, the italic style is read 4.9% slower than roman type (14–16 words per minute). This is why most literature, especially literature for early readers, is published using roman type.

Slanted manuscript can impair letter recognition

Educators have suspected that it would be beneficial for students to write and read the same style of alphabet. In other words, if children *read* vertical manuscript, they should also *write* vertical manuscript. Now it has been found that inconsistent alphabets may actually be detrimental to children's learning.

Researchers have found that slanted manuscript impairs the ability of some young children to recognize many letters. Some children who learn the slanted style alphabet find it difficult to recognize many of the traditional letterforms they see in books and environmental print. "[These children] consistently had difficulty identifying several letters, often making the same erroneous response to the same letter," the researchers reported. They concluded that slanted manuscript "creates substantially more letter recognition errors and causes more letter confusion than does the traditional style." (Kuhl & Dewitz, 1994).

Slanted manuscript does not help with transition

One of the benefits proposed by the creators of the slanted manuscript alphabet was that it made it easier for children to make the transition from manuscript to cursive writing. However, no difference in transition time has been found between the two styles of manuscript alphabets. In addition, the slanted style does not seem to enhance young children's production of cursive letters (Graham, 1992).

The slanted style of manuscript appeared to be a good idea. But educators should take a close look at what the research shows before adopting this style of alphabet. As one researcher has said, "Given the lack of supportive evidence and the practical problems involved in implementation, slanted manuscript letters cannot be recommended as a replacement for the traditional manuscript alphabet" (Graham, 1994).

> *"...slanted manuscript letters cannot be recommended as a replacement for the traditional manuscript alphabet."*

Farris, P.J. (1993). Learning to write the ABC's: A comparison of D'Nealian and Zaner-Bloser handwriting styles. *Indiana Reading Quarterly*, 25 (4), 26–33.

Graham, S. (1992). Issues in handwriting instruction. *Focus on Exceptional Children*, 25 (2).

Graham, S. (1994, Winter). Are slanted manuscript alphabets superior to the traditional manuscript alphabet? *Childhood Education*, 91–95.

Kuhl, D. & Dewitz, P. (1994, April). The effect of handwriting style on alphabet recognition. Paper presented at the annual meeting of the American Educational Research Association, New Orleans, LA.

Under your care . . .
your students receive the best possible attention everyday!

Now that you use *Zaner-Bloser Handwriting*, we want to be sure you get the attention you need to make your job more successful. We have many communication channels available to meet your needs: phone our Customer Service Department at 1-800-421-3018, visit our website at www.zaner-bloser.com, use the card below to write to our editors, and use the card at the bottom to join our Customer Care Club.

Zaner-Bloser cares!

If you have any questions or comments concerning Zaner-Bloser instructional materials or questions about the teaching of handwriting, you may use this card to write to us. We will be happy to assist you in any way possible.

_____

_____

_____

_____

_____

Ms., Mr., etc.	Name	Position	Grade Level(s)
School		School Address	
City		State	ZIP
( ) School Telephone		( ) After Hours Phone	( ) FAX

MH0327

Zaner-Bloser Customer Care Club

Join the Zaner-Bloser Customer Care Club and we'll make sure you stay up-to-date on current educational research and products. To enroll, you may return this card or call our Customer Care Club hotline at 1-800-387-2410. Upon enrollment, we'll get you started with a gift of information about teaching handwriting.

 **YES!** Please enroll me in the Zaner-Bloser Customer Care Club and send me the following pamphlet: **The Left-Handed Child in a Right-Handed World**

Zaner-Bloser

2200 W. Fifth Ave.
PO Box 16764
Columbus, OH
43216-6764

Visit our website:
www.zaner-bloser.com

Ms., Mr., etc.	Name	Position	Grade Level(s)
School		School Address	
City		State	ZIP
( ) School Telephone		( ) After Hours Phone	( ) FAX

Please Note: This program is for Zaner-Bloser customers only!

MH0327

Zaner-Bloser

Customer Service: 1-800-421-3018

Customer Care Club: 1-800-387-2410

Website: www.zaner-bloser.com

BUSINESS REPLY MAIL
FIRST CLASS MAIL   PERMIT NO. 295   COLUMBUS, OH

POSTAGE WILL BE PAID BY ADDRESSEE

Zaner-Bloser
2200 W 5TH AVE
PO BOX 16764
COLUMBUS OH 43272-4176

NO POSTAGE
NECESSARY
IF MAILED
IN THE
UNITED STATES

BUSINESS REPLY MAIL
FIRST CLASS MAIL   PERMIT NO. 295   COLUMBUS, OH

POSTAGE WILL BE PAID BY ADDRESSEE

Zaner-Bloser
2200 W 5TH AVE
PO BOX 16764
COLUMBUS OH 43272-4176

Meeting Students' Individual Handwriting Needs

The Left-Handed Student

With proper instruction and encouragement, left-handed students can write as well as right-handed students. Three important techniques assist the left-handed student in writing.

Paper Position

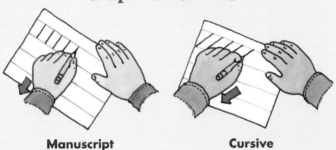

Manuscript   **Cursive**

For *manuscript writing,* the **lower right corner** of the paper should point toward the left of the body's mid-section.

For *cursive writing,* the **lower right corner** of the paper should point toward the body's midsection.

Downstrokes are pulled toward the left elbow.

Pencil Position

The top of the pencil should point toward the left elbow. The pen or pencil should be held at least one inch above the point. This allows students to see what they are writing.

Arm Position

Holding the left arm close to the body and keeping the hand below the line of writing prevents "hooking" the wrist and smearing the writing.

Students With Reversal Tendencies

• Downcurve
• Undercurve
• Slant
• Loop forward, undercurve

Directionality

A problem with directionality (moving from left to right across the page) interferes with a child's ability to form letters correctly and to write text that makes sense. To develop correct directionality, try these techniques:

• Provide opportunities for the child to write at the chalkboard within a confined area with frequent arrows as a reminder of left-to-right progression.
• Prepare sheets of paper on which the left edges and the beginning stroke of a letter, such as *b,* are colored green.

Letter Reversals

Determine which letters a student most often reverses. Make a list of these reversals and concentrate on them either on an individual basis or by grouping together the students who are reversing the same letters.

• Emphasize each step of the stroke description before the children write a letter.
• Provide a letter for tracing that has been colored according to stroke order. Repeat the stroke description with the children as they write the letter.
• Encourage the children to write the letter as they verbalize the stroke description.

Students With Other Special Needs

Success in handwriting is almost always a certainty if the initial instruction involves visual, auditory, and kinesthetic stimuli—a multisensory approach. Students need to develop a correct mental and motor image of the stroke, joining, letter, or word before they attempt to write. These techniques may help your students with special needs.

For the Kinesthetic Learner

- Walk out the letter strokes on the floor.
- Form letters in the air using full-arm movement.
- Make letter models with clay or string.
- Write strokes, letters, and joinings in sand.
- Use different writing instruments, such as crayons, markers, and varied sizes of pencils.
- Trace large strokes, letters, and joinings on the chalkboard and on paper—first with fingers, then with chalk or other media.
- Dip fingers in water and form letters and joinings on the chalkboard.

Remember that initial instruction, remediation, and maintenance for the student whose primary sensory modality is kinesthetic should be tactile, involving movement and the sense of touch.

For the Auditory Learner

- Verbalize each stroke in the letter as that letter is presented.
- Encourage the student to verbalize the letter strokes and to explain how strokes are alike and how they are different in the letterforms.
- Ask students to write random letters as you verbalize the strokes.
- Be consistent in the language you use to describe letters, strokes, shapes, and joinings.

Students whose primary sensory modality is auditory require instruction that enables them to listen and to verbalize.

For the Visual Learner

- Encourage students first to look at the letter as a whole and to ask themselves if the letter is tall or short, fat or skinny. Does all of the letter rest on the baseline, or is it a descender or a tall letter? How many and what kinds of strokes are in the letter?
- Have students look at each individual stroke carefully before they attempt to write the letter.

As a general rule, a student whose primary sensory modality is visual will have little difficulty in handwriting if instruction includes adequate visual stimuli.

For Learners With Attention Deficit Problems

Because they have difficulty focusing and maintaining attention, these students must concentrate on individual strokes in the letterforms. When they have learned the strokes, they can put them together to form letters, and then learn the joinings (in cursive) to write words.
- Give very short assignments.
- Supervise closely and give frequent encouragement.

Activities recommended for kinesthetic learners are appropriate for students with an attention deficit disorder.

General Coaching Tips for Teachers

- Teach a handwriting lesson daily, if possible, for no more than 15 minutes. Short, daily periods of instruction are preferable to longer, but less frequent, periods.
- Surround children with models of good handwriting. Set an example when you write on the chalkboard and on students' papers.
- Teach the letters through basic strokes.
- Emphasize one key to legibility at a time.
- Use appropriately ruled paper. Don't be afraid to increase the size of the grids for any student who is experiencing difficulty.
- Stress comfortable writing posture and pencil position. Increase the size of the pencil for students who "squeeze" the writing implement.
- Show the alternate method of holding the pencil, and allow students to choose the one that is better for them. (Refer to the alternate method shown on the Position Pages in the Teacher Edition.)
- Provide opportunities for children in the upper grades to use manuscript writing. Permit manuscript for some assignments, if children prefer manuscript to cursive.
- Encourage students with poor sustained motor control to use conventional manuscript, with frequent lifts, if continuous manuscript is difficult for them.

Zaner-Bloser
Handwriting
With a simplified alphabet

Author

Clinton S. Hackney

Contributing Authors

Pamela J. Farris
Janice T. Jones
Linda Leonard Lamme

Zaner-Bloser, Inc.
P.O. Box 16764
Columbus, Ohio 43216-6764

Teacher Edition Artists

Liz Callen; Denise & Fernando; Michael Grejniec; Rosekrans Hoffman; Diane Paterson; Andy San Diego; Troy Viss

Photos

John Lei

Author

Clinton S. Hackney, Ed.D.

Contributing Authors

Pamela J. Farris, Ph.D.
Janice T. Jones, M.A.
Linda Leonard Lamme, Ph.D.

Reviewers

Judy L. Bausch, Columbus, Georgia
Cherlynn Bruce, Conroe, Texas
Karen H. Burke, Director of Curriculum and Instruction, Bar Mills, Maine
Anne Chamberlin, Lynchburg, Virginia
Carol J. Fuhler, Flagstaff, Arizona
Deborah D. Gallagher, Gainesville, Florida
Kathleen Harrington, Redford, Michigan
Rebecca James, East Greenbush, New York
Gerald R. Maeckelbergh, Principal, Blaine, Minnesota
Bessie B. Peabody, Principal, East St. Louis, Illinois

Marilyn S. Petruska, Coraopolis, Pennsylvania
Sharon Ralph, Nashville, Tennessee
Linda E. Ritchie, Birmingham, Alabama
Roberta Hogan Royer, North Canton, Ohio
Marion Redmond Starks, Baltimore, Maryland
Elizabeth J. Taglieri, Lake Zurich, Illinois
Claudia Williams, Lewisburg, West Virginia

Credits

Art: Liz Callen: 3, 26–27, 29, 42–43, 45, 64–65, 71, 86–87, 101, 106; Gloria Elliott: 5, 16, 58, 96; Michael Grejniec: 1, 3, 6–7, 20–21, 34–35, 37, 44, 50–53, 56–57, 72–73, 82–83, 94, 99, 110; Rosekrans Hoffman: 3, 30–31, 46–47, 58, 62–63, 76–77, 85, 90, 100, 105; Andy San Diego: 3, 5, 16–19, 32–33, 48–49, 59–61, 70, 80–81, 84, 92–93, 102; Troy Viss: 3, 12–13, 24–25, 28, 36, 40–41, 66–67, 78–79, 88–89, 96, 104, 108–109; John Wallner: 22–23, 38–39, 68–69, 74–75, 91, 103, 107

Photos: John Lei/OPC: 8–9, 97; Stephen Ogilvy: 3–4, 7, 10–11, 13–15, 20–21, 24–25, 29, 32–33, 36, 38–39, 42, 46–47, 50, 55, 56–57, 60–63, 65–68, 71–73, 75–77, 79–83, 86–89, 91–93, 95, 97–99, 101, 105, 107–109, 110

Developed by Kirchoff/Wohlberg, Inc., in cooperation with Zaner-Bloser Publishers
Cover illustration by Michael Grejniec

ISBN 0-88085-948-2

CONTENTS

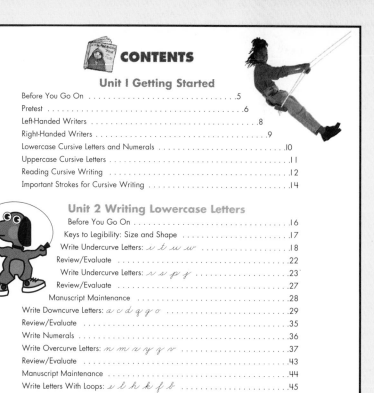

cool

If you can read this word, you're ready to write in cursive.

In cursive writing, letters are joined to other letters. In this book, you will learn how to write cursive letters, how to join the letters to write words, and how to space the words to write sentences. You will learn how to make your writing easy to read.

5

Unit Summary
This page tells students about the content, organization, and focus of the book. Students begin by taking a pretest to assess current ability. The lessons that follow review what students need to know to develop good handwriting skills.

Preview the Book
Preview the book with students, calling attention to its organization.

- Unit I presents handwriting basics.
- Unit 2 introduces lowercase cursive letters grouped by common strokes.
- Unit 3 introduces uppercase cursive letters grouped by common strokes.
- Unit 4 provides a variety of opportunities for students to apply what they've learned.

Point out that students will evaluate their handwriting frequently. Set up a portfolio for each student to assess individual progress throughout the year.

Introduction to Cursive Writing
The following are some criteria to help determine whether a student is ready for cursive writing.

Reading Level Does the student show reading proficiency near grade level?

Manuscript Mastery Is the student able to write legibly in manuscript?

Cursive Letter Recognition Is the student able to recognize and identify all cursive letters?

Cursive Word Reading Is the student able to read cursive words?

Grouping of Letters Is the student able to group letters according to size, shape, beginning stroke, and ending stroke?

Understanding of Terminology Does the student understand the terms for cursive handwriting?

Understanding of Slant Does the student understand that slant is determined by paper position, the direction in which the downstrokes are pulled, and the shifting of the paper as the writing space is filled?

Practice Masters for Unit 1

Maintaining Manuscript
As students prepare for the introduction of cursive writing, it is important to remind them that the maintenance of their manuscript skills will still be stressed. Students should realize that cursive may become the style they use the most, but that their manuscript skills will always be useful.

Have students use the poem as a model for writing on page 7. Ask them to keep their pretests in writing portfolios for comparison with their posttests later in the year. You may want the students to write the pretest periodically to provide samples of their improvement. Students who learned cursive handwriting in second grade may choose to write the pretest in cursive. (visual)

Pretest

So Much
I have so much to say.
And so much to write.
I want every word
To be written just right!

So Much
I have so much to say.
And so much to write.
I want every word
To be written just right!

So Much
I have so much to say.
And so much to write.
I want every word
To be written just right!

So Much

I have so much to say
And so much to write.
I want every word
To be written just right!

So Much
I have so much to say.
And so much to write.
I want every word
To be written just right!

6

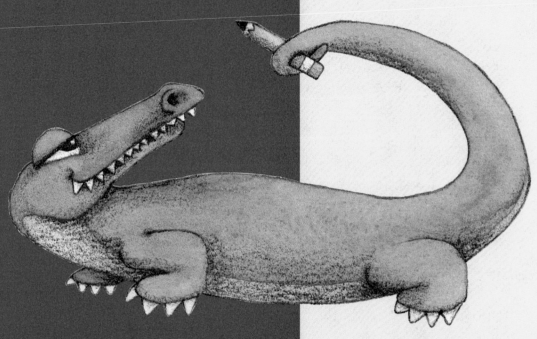

So Much
I have so much to say
And so much to write.
I want every word
To be written just right!!

Write the poem in your best handwriting.

Circle your best line of writing.

7

EVALUATE

As students write, monitor and informally assess their performance. Then guide them through the self-evaluation process. Meet individually with students to help them assess their handwriting. Ask them how they would like to improve their writing. (visual, auditory)

COACHING HINT: SELF-EVALUATION

Self-evaluation is an important step in the handwriting process. By identifying their own strengths and weaknesses, students become independent learners. The steps in the self-evaluation process are as follows:

I. Question
Students should ask themselves questions such as these: "Is my slant correct?" "Do my letters rest on the baseline?"

2. Compare
Students should compare their handwriting to correct models.

3. Evaluate
Students should determine strengths and weaknesses in their handwriting based on the keys to legibility.

4. Diagnose
Students should diagnose the cause of any difficulties. Possible causes include incorrect paper or pencil position, inconsistent pressure on pencil, and incorrect strokes.

5. Improve
Self-evaluation should include a means of improvement through additional instruction and continued practice. (visual, auditory, kinesthetic)

LEFT-HANDED WRITERS RIGHT-HANDED WRITERS

Suggest that students refer to these pages throughout the year as a reminder of proper posture and correct paper and pencil position. Demonstrate correct positions for both left-handed and right-handed writers. Then ask students to place a sheet of paper in the proper position on their desks, pick up a pencil, and write their names. (visual, auditory, kinesthetic)

COACHING HINT: LEFT-HANDED WRITERS

You may wish to group left-handed students together for instruction if you can do so without calling attention to the practice. They should be seated to the left of the chalkboard.

If you are left-handed . . .

Sit up tall. Place both arms on the table. Keep your feet flat on the floor. This way, your body will be well balanced.

Hold your pencil with your first two fingers and your thumb. Point the pencil toward your left elbow.

Your paper should slant with the lower right corner pointing toward you. Pull your downstrokes toward your left elbow. Then you can make your writing slant the way you want it to.

Left-Handed Writers

8

PENCIL POSITION

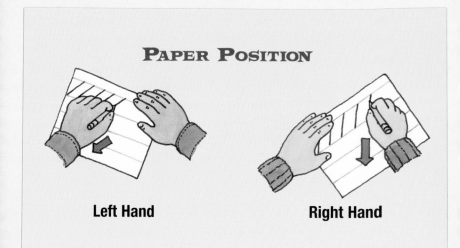

Rest the pencil near your big knuckle.

Hold the pencil with your first two fingers and thumb.

Point the pencil toward your left elbow.

Point the pencil toward your right shoulder

Bend your thumb.

Left Hand

Rest your last two fingers on the paper.

Right Hand

PAPER POSITION

Left Hand

Right Hand

Right-Handed Writers

EVALUATE

Check for correct paper and pencil position. The Zaner-Bloser Writing Frame can be used to help improve hand position. (visual, kinesthetic)

COACHING HINT: USE OF THE CHALKBOARD

You and your students can follow these suggestions for writing on the chalkboard.

Left-handed writers. Stand in front of the writing lines and pull the downstrokes to the left elbow. The elbow is bent, and the writing is done at a comfortable height. Step to the right often to maintain correct slant.

Right-handed writers. Stand to the left of the writing lines and pull the downstrokes toward the midsection of the body. The elbow is bent, and the writing is done at a comfortable height. Step to the right often to maintain correct slant. (visual, kinesthetic)

Children who have difficulty with the traditional pencil position may prefer the alternate method of holding the pencil between the first and second fingers.

LOWERCASE CURSIVE LETTERS AND NUMERALS

Students can use the chart on this page to identify lowercase cursive letters and numerals. (visual, auditory)

COACHING HINT

Review with students the use of guidelines for correct letter formation. Draw guidelines on the chalkboard, using colored chalk to identify the headline, midline, and baseline. Invite volunteers to write words on the guidelines. (visual, auditory, kinesthetic)

Lowercase Cursive Letters and Numerals

aa   bb   cc   dd   ee   ff   gg
hh   ii   jj   kk   ll   mm   nn
oo   pp   qq   rr   ss   tt   uu
vv   ww   xx   yy   zz

1 2 3 4 5 6 7 8 9 10

Circle the lowercase cursive letters that are in your name.

How are these manuscript and cursive words different?

handwriting

handwriting

Uppercase Cursive Letters

A*a* B*b* C*c* D*d* E*e* F*f* G*g*
H*h* I*i* J*j* K*k* L*l* M*m* N*n*
O*o* P*p* Q*q* R*r* S*s* T*t* U*u*
V*v* W*w* X*x* Y*y* Z*z* !*!*   ?*?*

Circle your cursive initials.

Circle the cursive letter that begins the name of your state.

How are these sentences different?

Ben moved to Tampa.

Ben moved to Tampa.

11

UPPERCASE CURSIVE LETTERS

Students can use the chart on this page to identify uppercase cursive letters and punctuation. (visual, auditory)

COACHING HINT

Give half the students manuscript letter cards and the other half the corresponding cursive letter cards. On a signal, have them scramble to locate their partner. Repeat several times to reinforce the identification of the cursive letters. (visual)

EVALUATE

Poll students to find out which cursive letters and numerals are most difficult for them to read. Discuss possible reasons for this difficulty. Then ask students to describe the similarities and differences between the manuscript and cursive letters and numerals. (auditory)

READING CURSIVE WRITING

Students can use this lesson to practice reading cursive writing.

Reading Cursive Writing

Read the card. Write the words in manuscript under each cursive phrase.

Happy birthday.

Happy birthday.

Happy birthday to you.

How old are you?

How old are you?

How old are you now?

I am 8.

I am 9.

How old is she?

13

EVALUATE

Ask students to describe the similarities and differences between the cursive writing they read and the manuscript writing they wrote. (auditory)

IMPORTANT STROKES FOR CURSIVE WRITING

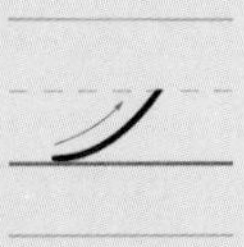

UNDERCURVE
Touch the baseline; curve under and up to the midline.

UNDERCURVE
Touch the baseline; curve under and up to the headline.

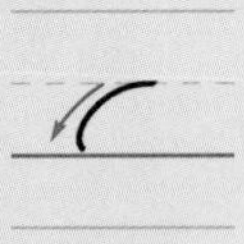

DOWNCURVE
Touch the midline; curve left and down to the baseline.

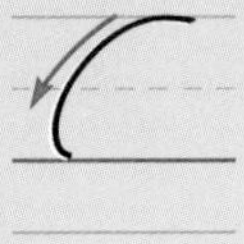

DOWNCURVE
Touch the headline; curve left and down to the baseline.

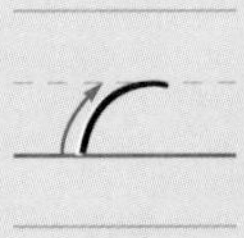

OVERCURVE
Touch the baseline; curve up and right to the midline.

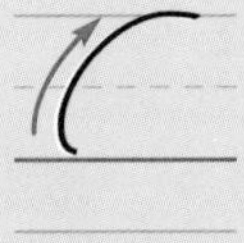

OVERCURVE
Touch the baseline; curve up and right to the headline.

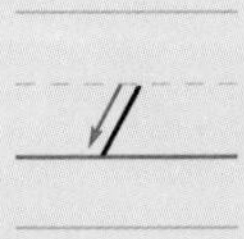

SLANT
Touch the midline; slant left to the baseline.

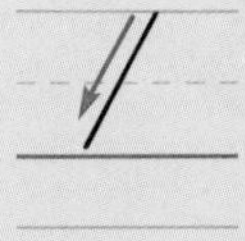

SLANT
Touch the headline; slant left to the baseline.

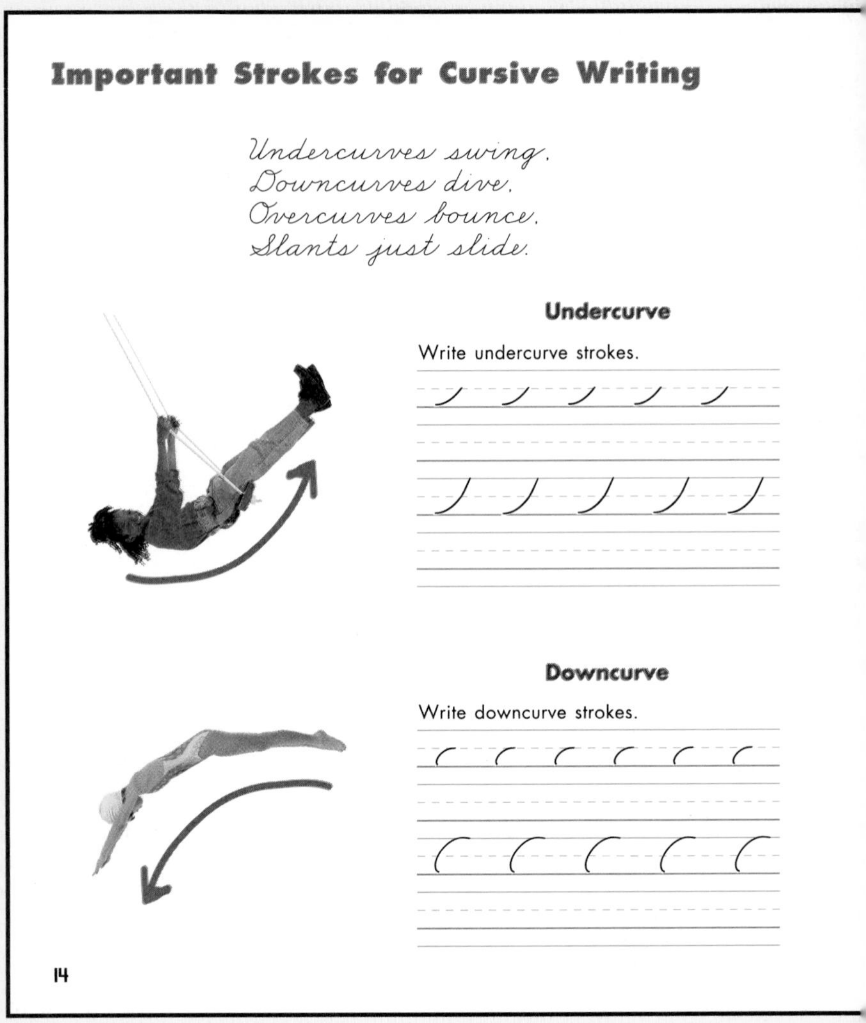

Important Strokes for Cursive Writing

Undercurves swing.
Downcurves dive.
Overcurves bounce.
Slants just slide.

Undercurve
Write undercurve strokes.

Downcurve
Write downcurve strokes.

14

MODEL THE WRITING

Model the two sizes of each stroke on guidelines. Invite students to say the names as they write the strokes in the air. Point out that cursive letters are formed from these basic strokes. Suggest that students name the strokes as they write them to complete the page. (visual, auditory, kinesthetic)

Undercurve, downcurve.
Overcurve, slant.
As you write cursive letters,
Remember this chant.

Overcurve

Write overcurve strokes.

Slant

Write slant strokes.

15

EVALUATE

To help students evaluate their writing, ask questions such as these:
Do your undercurve and overcurve strokes start at the baseline?
Do your downcurve strokes end at the baseline?
Are your slant strokes pulled toward the baseline? (visual, auditory)

Provide sheets of newspaper and a dark crayon for each student. Let students tape their newspapers to a chalkboard or wall and practice their strokes in large, sweeping motions. Encourage them to practice each stroke several times and to feel the motion that each one involves. (kinesthetic, visual)

You've got to start somewhere!

Writing Lowercase Letters

Begin here. Circle the lowercase letters that are written in cursive.

a b *c* *d* e *f* g

h *i* *j* *k* l m n

o *p* *q* *r* s t *u*

v w *x* *y* z

In the following pages, you will write all the lowercase letters in cursive. You will pay attention to the size and shape of letters to help make your writing easy to read.

16

UNIT SUMMARY

This page tells students about the content, organization, and focus of the unit. Then students are introduced to the first two keys to legibility for lowercase letters: size and shape. The lessons that follow emphasize lowercase letter formation and joinings. Students evaluate their work and circle their best letter in each lesson.

PREVIEW THE UNIT

Preview the unit with students, calling attention to these features:

- letter models in both manuscript and cursive
- cursive letter models with numbered directional arrows
- guidelines for student writing directly beneath handwriting models
- opportunities to evaluate lowercase letter size and shape
- a cursive numerals lesson
- writing activities for manuscript maintenance
- review lessons of lowercase letters grouped by initial stroke

Keys to Legibility: Size and Shape

Help make your writing easy to read.
Pay attention to the size and shape of lowercase letters.

Tall letters touch the headline.

Short letters touch the midline.

Letters with descenders go below the baseline.

Look at the letters below. Circle the green letters that are the correct size and shape.

17

KEYS TO LEGIBILITY: SIZE AND SHAPE

Tell students that all the letters of the same size should be even in height. Tall letters (those a full space high) touch the headline. Short letters (letters one-half space high) touch the midline. Letters with descenders extend below the baseline.

PRACTICE MASTERS FOR UNIT 2

COACHING HINT: SIZE

Demonstrate for students the technique of drawing a horizontal line with a ruler along the tops of letters to show proper size. Have students come to the chalkboard and use colored chalk and a ruler to draw horizontal lines along the top of a group of tall letters and a group of short letters. Have students practice this technique periodically to evaluate their own letter size in all subject areas. (kinesthetic, visual)

COACHING HINT: SHAPE

Review with students the use of the guidelines for correct letter formation. As you demonstrate on the chalkboard, have students do the following on practice paper:

• Draw over the baseline with a red crayon.
• Draw over the headline and midline with a blue crayon. (kinesthetic, visual, auditory)

Undercurve
Slant, undercurve, (lift)
Dot

PRACTICE

Let students use laminated writing cards or slates to practice writing the letter.

COACHING HINT

Students' progress in handwriting is greater when short, intensive periods of instruction are used, approximately fifteen minutes for a lesson.

Note: In each Evaluate section, the letterforms illustrate common problems in letter formation.

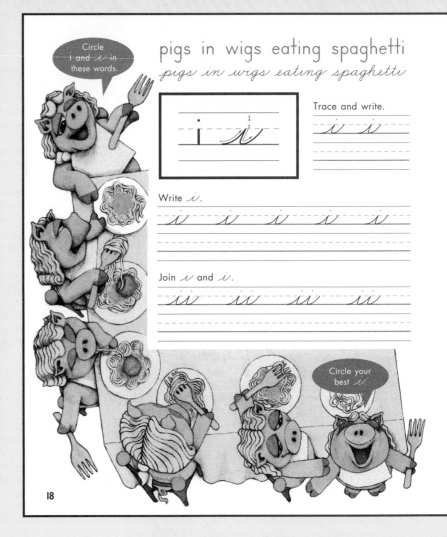

pigs in wigs eating spaghetti

pigs in wigs eating spaghetti

Circle i and *i* in these words.

Trace and write.

Write *i*.

Join *i* and *i*.

Circle your best *i*.

18

PRACTICE MASTER 3

MODEL THE WRITING

Write **i** on guidelines as you say the stroke descriptions. To help students visualize the letter, model **i** in the air. Have students echo the stroke descriptions as they write **i** in the air with you. Ask questions such as these:
What are the three strokes in **i**? (undercurve, slant, undercurve)
Where is the dot? (halfway between the headline and the midline)

EVALUATE

To help students evaluate their writing, ask questions such as these:
Does your letter rest on the baseline?
Does your first stroke end at the midline?
Does your last stroke end at the midline? (visual, auditory)

CORRECTIVE STRATEGY

i   NOT   *i*

Pull the slant stroke toward the baseline and pause before making the undercurve ending.

a tower of tigers in tutus

a tower of tigers in tutus

Circle **t** and *t* in these words.

Trace and write.

t t

Write *t*.

t t t t t

Join *t* and other letters.

tt tt tt tt

Circle your best *t*.

ti ti ti ti

Write the word *it*.

it it it it

19

Undercurve
Slant, undercurve, (lift)
Slide right

PRACTICE
Let students use laminated writing cards or slates to practice writing the letter.

WRITE AWAY
Provide sheets of newspaper and a dark crayon for each student. Let students tape their newspaper to a wall and practice their strokes in large, sweeping motions. Have students use strokes to create pictures.

MODEL THE WRITING
Write **t** on guidelines as you say the stroke descriptions. To help students visualize the letter, model **t** in the air. Have students echo the stroke descriptions as they write **t** in the air with you. Ask questions such as these:
Where does the first undercurve end? *(at the headline)*
Where does the second undercurve end? *(at the midline)*

EVALUATE

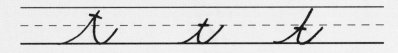

To help students evaluate their writing, ask questions such as these:
Does your first undercurve end at the headline?
Is your slant stroke pulled toward the baseline?
Is your **t** crossed above the midline? (visual, auditory)

CORRECTIVE STRATEGY

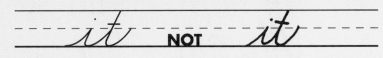

it **NOT** *it*

Swing wide on the undercurve to undercurve joining.

Name

Position the paper correctly. Write the letter.

t t t t t t t

Look at the large letter carefully. Make sure the paper is in the correct position. Trace the letter.

t t t t

Write the large letter. Follow the dots.

t t t t

Position the paper correctly. Write the letter and the joinings.

t t t t t t t

tt tt tt ti ti ti

EVALUATE Circle your best letter. Circle your best joining.
PRACTICE MASTER 4   Copyright © Zaner-Bloser, Inc.

PRACTICE MASTER 4

Undercurve
Slant, undercurve
Slant, undercurve

PRACTICE

Let students use laminated writing cards or slates to practice writing the letter.

COACHING HINT

Students can evaluate slant by drawing lines through the slant strokes of their letters. The lines should be parallel and should show the correct degree of forward slant.

Name

Position the paper correctly. Write the letter.

Look at the large letter carefully. Make sure the paper is in the correct position. Trace the letter.

Write the large letter. Follow the dots.

Position the paper correctly. Write the letter and the joinings.

EVALUATE Circle your best letter. Circle your best joining.
Copyright © Zaner-Bloser, Inc.   PRACTICE MASTER 5

PRACTICE MASTER 5

20

Circle
u and *uu* in
these words:

unicorns with ukuleles
unicorns with ukuleles

Trace and write.

u *uu*

Write *u*.

Join *u* and other letters.

ut   ut   tu   tu   uit

Write words with *u*.

tut   tutu

Circle your best *u*

20

MODEL THE WRITING

Write **u** on guidelines as you say the stroke descriptions. To help students visualize the letter, model **u** in the air. Have students echo the stroke descriptions as they write **u** in the air with you. Ask questions such as these:
How many slant strokes are in **u**? *(two)*
How many undercurves are in **u**? *(three)*

EVALUATE

To help students evaluate their writing, ask questions such as these:
Does your **u** begin at the baseline?
Does your **u** end at the midline?
Is your **u** about the same width as the model? (visual, auditory)

CORRECTIVE STRATEGY

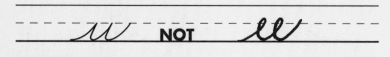

Pause before writing the slant strokes.

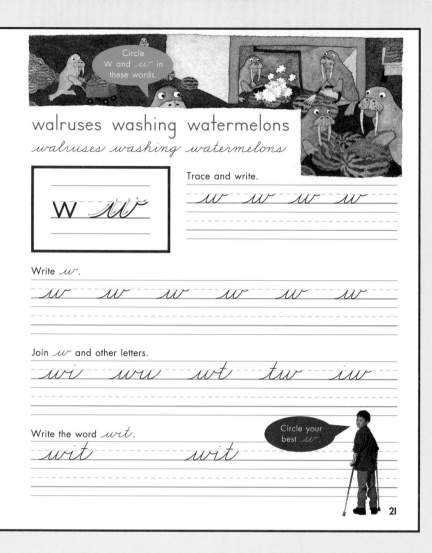

Circle W and *w* in these words

walruses washing watermelons
walruses washing watermelons

Trace and write.

W *w*

w w w w

Write *w*.

w w w w w w

Join *w* and other letters.

wi wu wt tw iw

Write the word *wit*.

wit wit

Circle your best *w*.

21

Undercurve
Slant, undercurve
Slant, undercurve
Checkstroke

PRACTICE

Let students use laminated writing cards or slates to practice writing the letter.

WRITE AWAY

Ask students to create a food or drink product they would like. Have them design a label for it and write a word (in manuscript or cursive) that could be used to describe it. Ask them to use words with **w** in them.

Name

Position the paper correctly. Write the letter.

w w w w w w w

Look at the large letter carefully. Make sure the paper is in the correct position. Trace the letter.

w w w

Write the large letter. Follow the dots.

w w w

Position the paper correctly. Write the letter and the joinings.

w w w w w w w

wi wu wt tw

EVALUATE Circle your best letter. Circle your best joining.
PRACTICE MASTER 6   Copyright © Zaner-Bloser, Inc.

PRACTICE MASTER 6

MODEL THE WRITING

Write **w** on guidelines as you say the stroke descriptions. Have students echo the stroke descriptions as they write **w** in the air with you. Ask questions such as these:
How is **w** like **u**? *(Both begin with an undercurve; both have slant strokes; both have three undercurves.)*
How is the last stroke in **w** different from the last stroke in **u**? *(The letter **w** ends with a checkstroke.)*

EVALUATE

w w

To help students evaluate their writing, ask questions such as these:
Are your slant strokes pulled down straight to the baseline?
Does your checkstroke begin and end at the midline? (visual, auditory)

CORRECTIVE STRATEGY

wi **NOT** *wi*

In the checkstroke to undercurve joining, it is best to deepen the retrace a little before swinging into the undercurve of the next letter.

REFOCUS

Review the letters **i**, **t**, **u**, and **w** by writing them on the chalkboard. Ask questions such as these:

What is the same about all four letters? *(All begin with an undercurve.)*

Which letter ends differently from the others? *(w)*

How does it end? *(with a checkstroke)*

How do the others end? *(with an undercurve)*

Ask volunteers to call out various combinations of two of the four letters. Demonstrate the joining method for each pair. Emphasize the different stroke needed when **w** is the initial letter—checkstroke to undercurve.

COACHING HINT: LEFT-HANDED WRITERS

Seat left-handed students to the left side of the chalkboard.

WRITE AWAY

Ask students to write and illustrate a short story about a pig, a tiger, a unicorn, or a walrus. Participate by telling your own short story about one of these animals.

22

Review

Write these letter joinings.

ti   tu   tw   twi

ui   ut   uit

Circle your best joining.

wi   wt   wu

Circle your best word.

Write these words.

it   wit   tut   tutu

22

EVALUATE

To help students evaluate their writing, ask questions such as these:

Is your **i** dotted?

Does your **t** touch the headline?

Are your joinings formed correctly?

Is your **wu** joining legible? *(visual, auditory)*

rhinos riding rubber rafts
rhinos riding rubber rafts

Circle **r** and *r* in these words.

r | *r*

Trace and write.

Write *r*.

Join *r* and other letters.

ri   ru   rt   wr

wri   ir   urt

Write words with *r*.

rut   writ

Circle your best *r*.

23

Undercurve
Slant right
Slant, undercurve

PRACTICE

Let students use laminated writing cards or slates to practice writing the letter.

COACHING HINT

Use the overhead projector to project **r** onto the chalkboard. Ask students to wet their index fingers in a cup of water and to trace over the letter on the chalkboard. (kinesthetic, visual)

MODEL THE WRITING

Write **r** on guidelines as you say the stroke descriptions. To help students visualize the letter, model **r** in the air. Have students echo the stroke descriptions as they write **r** in the air with you. Ask questions such as these:
How does **r** begin? *(with an undercurve)*
What stroke follows the first undercurve? *(slant right)*
How does **r** end? *(with an undercurve)*

EVALUATE

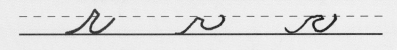

To help students evaluate their writing, ask questions such as these:
Does your first undercurve end at the midline?
Does your **r** have correct slant?
Are your lines smooth and even? (visual, auditory)

CORRECTIVE STRATEGY

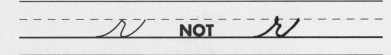

r   **NOT**   *r*

Pause after the first undercurve and slant right.

Name

Position the paper correctly. Write the letter.

Look at the large letter carefully. Make sure the paper is in the correct position. Trace the letter.

Write the large letter. Follow the dots.

Position the paper correctly. Write the letter and the joinings.

EVALUATE Circle your best letter. Circle your best joining.
Copyright © Zaner-Bloser, Inc.   **PRACTICE MASTER 7**

PRACTICE MASTER 7

**Undercurve
Retrace, curve down
and back
Undercurve**

PRACTICE

Let students use laminated writing cards or slates to practice writing the letter.

COACHING HINT

Draw writing lines on one side of 9" x 12" pieces of oak tag, and laminate one for each student. Students can use these as "slates" by practicing their handwriting with a wipe-off crayon. The reverse side can be used for such things as letter activities. (visual, kinesthetic)

Name

Position the paper correctly. Write the letter.

Look at the large letter carefully. Make sure the paper is in the correct position. Trace the letter.

Write the large letter. Follow the dots.

Position the paper correctly. Write the letter and the words.

sit   wrist   rust

EVALUATE Circle your best letter. Circle your best word.

PRACTICE MASTER 8   Copyright © Zaner-Bloser, Inc.

PRACTICE MASTER 8

24

Circle S and s in these words.

storks in striped sweaters
storks in striped sweaters

S   Trace and write.

s   s   s   s   s

Write *s*.

s   s   s   s   s   s   s

Join *s* and other letters.

si   su   st   sw   rs

Write words with *s*.

stir   suit   its

Circle your best *s*.

24

MODEL THE WRITING

Write **s** on guidelines as you say the stroke descriptions. Have students echo the stroke descriptions as they write **s** in the air with you. Ask questions such as these:
How is **s** like **r**? *(Both begin and end with an undercurve.)*
How are they different? *(After the first undercurve, **s** has a retrace followed by a curve down and back; **r** has a slant right stroke.)*

EVALUATE

s   s   s

To help students evaluate their writing, ask questions such as these:
Is the bottom of your **s** closed?
Does your **s** end at the midline?
Is your **s** about the same width as the model? (visual, auditory)

CORRECTIVE STRATEGY

s   **NOT**   *s*

Be sure the final undercurve touches the baseline.

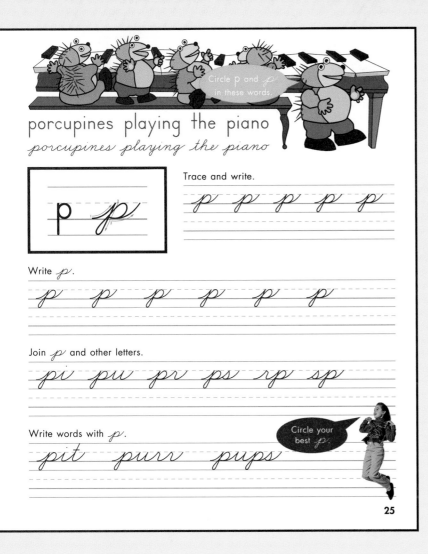

porcupines playing the piano
porcupines playing the piano

Circle p and *p* in these words.

Trace and write.

p *p*   *p p p p p*

Write *p*.

p p p p p p

Join *p* and other letters.

pi pu pr ps rp sp

Write words with *p*.

pit purr pups

Circle your best *p*.

25

Undercurve
Slant, loop back
Overcurve, curve back
Undercurve

PRACTICE
Let students use laminated writing cards or slates to practice writing the letter.

WRITE AWAY
Challenge students to write words using the letters **i, t, u, w, r, s,** and **p.** Some students may want to try using cursive letters, experimenting with letters they want to use but have not yet been taught. Others may prefer to use manuscript.

MODEL THE WRITING
Write **p** on guidelines as you say the stroke descriptions. To help students visualize the letter, model **p** in the air. Have students echo the stroke descriptions as they write **p** in the air with you. Ask questions such as these:
Where does the beginning undercurve end? *(at the midline)*
Where does the loop close? *(near the baseline)*

EVALUATE

p   p   p

To help students evaluate their writing, ask questions such as these:
Does your beginning undercurve end at the midline?
Does your loop fill the descender space?
Does your slant loop to the left? (visual, auditory)

CORRECTIVE STRATEGY

p   **NOT**   *p*

End with an undercurve.

Name

Position the paper correctly. Write the letter.

p p p p p p p

Look at the large letter carefully. Make sure the paper is in the correct position. Trace the letter.

p p p

Write the large letter. Follow the dots.

p p p

Position the paper correctly. Write the letter and the words.

p p p p p p

tip spit put

EVALUATE Circle your best letter. Circle your best word.

Copyright © Zaner-Bloser, Inc.   **PRACTICE MASTER 9**

PRACTICE MASTER 9

25

Undercurve
Slant
Loop back, overcurve,
   (lift)
Dot

PRACTICE

Let students use laminated writing cards or slates to practice writing the letter.

COACHING HINT

A good book to read to students who are just starting cursive writing is *Muggie Maggie* by Beverly Cleary. (auditory)

PRACTICE MASTER 10

26

Circle j and *j* in these words.

jumping jaguars in pajamas
jumping jaguars in pajamas

Trace and write.

Write *j*.

Join *j* and other letters.

ji   jit   ju   uj

jui   jus   jur

Circle your best *j*

Write words with *j*.

jut   just   juts

26

MODEL THE WRITING

Write **j** on guidelines as you say the stroke descriptions. To help students visualize the letter, model **j** in the air. Have students write **j** in the air with you. Ask questions such as these:
Where does **j** begin? *(at the baseline)*
Where does the overcurve end? *(at the midline)*
Where is the dot? *(halfway between the headline and the midline)*

EVALUATE

To help students evaluate their writing, ask questions such as these:
Is your slant stroke pulled through the baseline?
Does your loop close at the baseline?
Does your **j** end with an overcurve? (visual, auditory)

CORRECTIVE STRATEGY

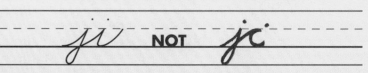

In the overcurve to undercurve joining, the overcurve ending stops at the baseline to blend with the undercurve beginning.

Review

r   *s*   *p*   *j*

Write these letter joinings.

rs   *rp*   *sp*   *pr*   *ju*

Circle your best joining.

Write these words.

sip   *tip*   *trip*   *suit*

just   *rust*   *spur*

Circle your best word.

wrist   *twists*

27

Review the letters **r**, **s**, **p**, and **j** by asking questions such as these:
How do all the letters begin? *(with an undercurve)*
Which of these letters ends differently? *(The j ends with an overcurve.)*
Which letters have a descender? *(p, j)*

Review the joining techniques by writing the following combinations on the chalkboard. Say the strokes as you write them.

ji	**tr**	**uw**	**sp**
st	**wi**	**ju**	**wr**

Have students write each combination three times on paper. Suggest they underline their best joining.

COACHING HINT: LEFT-HANDED WRITERS

You might want to group left-handed students together for handwriting lessons.

WRITE AWAY

Ask students to imagine that a porcupine could talk. Have them write a question they would like to ask a porcupine. Participate by asking a question you would like to ask a porcupine.

EVALUATE

To help students evaluate their writing, ask questions such as these:
Are your joinings formed correctly?
Do **r**, **s**, **p**, and **j** touch the midline?
Do the descenders in **p** and **j** fill the descender space? (visual, auditory)

MANUSCRIPT MAINTENANCE: SHAPE

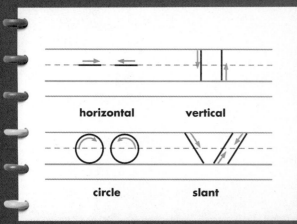

horizontal   **vertical**

circle   **slant**

Review with students the shape of manuscript letters by demonstrating the four kinds of lines that are used in writing manuscript letters. Provide opportunities to practice the formation of each manuscript letter on the hand-writing guidelines.

COACHING HINT
If a circle in a letter comes before the vertical line, write a backward circle, as in **a**. If a vertical line in a letter comes before the circle, write a forward circle, as in **b**. (visual)

WRITE AWAY
Ask students to use their best manuscript to write a paragraph describing their observations about the use of manuscript writing in the environment. Participate by naming a few uses, such as supermarket signs, billboards, and street signs.

Manuscript Maintenance: Compound Words

Join each word in the first column with a word in the second column to form a new word.

ant — shoe
dragon — fish
grass — house
cow — eater
jelly — neck
horse — hopper
turtle — fly
dog — hand

Write the new words in your best manuscript.

anteater   dragonfly   grasshopper   cowhand

jellyfish   horseshoe   turtleneck   doghouse

EVALUATE
To help students evaluate their writing, ask questions such as these:
Are your horizontal and vertical lines straight?
Are your backward and forward circles round?
Are your slant right and slant left lines written correctly? (visual, auditory)

MAINTAINING MANUSCRIPT
Permit students to use manuscript for creative writing, spelling assignments, and tests if they choose to do so.

Give a weekly assignment that requires manuscript, such as filling out forms, map study, charts, preparing labels and captions, crossword puzzles, and making posters.

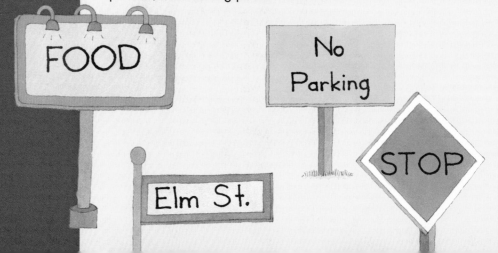

FOOD

No Parking

STOP

Elm St.

Circle **a** and *a* in these words.

anteaters in armor

anteaters in armor

Trace and write.

a   a   a   a

Write *a*.

a   a   a   a   a   a   a

Join *a* and other letters.

ai   ap   arp   ast   wa

Write words with *a*.

Circle your best *a*.

air   jar   upstairs

29

MODEL THE WRITING

Write **a** on guidelines as you say the stroke descriptions. To help students visualize the letter, model **a** in the air. Have students echo the stroke descriptions as they write **a** in the air with you. Ask questions such as these:

Where does the downcurve stroke begin? (*just below the midline*)

Where does **a** end? (*at the midline*)

Name the strokes in **a**. (*downcurve, undercurve, slant, undercurve*)

EVALUATE

a   a

To help students evaluate their writing, ask questions such as these:

Is your **a** closed?

Does your **a** end at the midline? (visual, auditory)

CORRECTIVE STRATEGY

a **NOT** *a*

Pull the slant stroke toward the baseline.

Downcurve
Undercurve
Slant, undercurve

PRACTICE

Let students use laminated writing cards or slates to practice writing the letter.

COACHING HINT

As students continue the transition from manuscript to cursive, they may find that maintaining correct spacing between letters is difficult. The joining stroke between letters must be wide enough to allow for good spacing. The exercise below will reinforce both fluent strokes and good spacing.

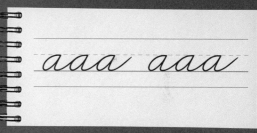

aaa aaa

Name

Write.

a   a   a   a   a

a   a   a   a   a   a

ai ap a arp ast wa

war pat waist

paws pair straw

raw stairs wait

Write your own words.

EVALUATE Circle your best letter. Circle your best joining. Circle your best word.
Copyright © Zaner-Bloser, Inc.   **PRACTICE MASTER II**

PRACTICE MASTER II

29

**Downcurve
Undercurve**

PRACTICE

Let students use laminated writing cards or slates to practice writing the letter.

COACHING HINT

Provide a shallow tray or box lid with a thin layer of sand in it. Allow students to form **c** and other letters in the sand. (kinesthetic)

```
Name _____

Write.
c  c  c  c  c  c  c  c
c  c  c  c  c  c  c  c
ca  ci  cu  scr  ct
cats  circus  cart
act  crust  attic
can  cast  scrap

Write your own words.

EVALUATE Circle your best letter. Circle your best joining. Circle your best word.
PRACTICE MASTER 12          Copyright © Zaner-Bloser, Inc.
```

PRACTICE MASTER 12

30

Circle c and c in these words.

cats on a cable car
cats on a cable car

Trace and write.

c   c   c   c

Write c.

c   c   c   c   c   c

Join c and other letters.

ca ci cu scr ct

Write words with c.

circus   cactus

cats   scrap   act

30

MODEL THE WRITING

Write **c** on guidelines as you say the stroke descriptions. To help students visualize the letter, model **c** in the air. Have students echo the stroke descriptions as they write **c** in the air with you. Ask questions such as these:
Where does **c** begin? *(below the midline)*
How does **c** end? *(with an undercurve)*

EVALUATE

c   c   c

To help students evaluate their writing, ask questions such as these:
Does your **c** have correct slant?
Does your **c** begin below the midline?
Does your **c** end at the midline? *(visual, auditory)*

CORRECTIVE STRATEGY

ci   NOT   ci

Swing wide on the undercurve to undercurve joining.

dancing dogs in derbies
dancing dogs in derbies

Trace and write.

Write *d*.

Join *d* and other letters.

Write words with *d*.

card aid add

Circle *d* and *d* in these words.

Circle your best *d*.

31

Downcurve
Undercurve
Slant, undercurve

PRACTICE

Let students use laminated writing cards or slates to practice writing the letter.

WRITE AWAY

Challenge students to use the letters **i, t, u, w, r, s, p, j, a, c,** and **d** to write rhyming words for *jar, sip, up, sad,* and *cat* by substituting the initial letter. Many children will still wish to use manuscript writing. Others may want to experiment with cursive writing.

MODEL THE WRITING

Write **d** on guidelines as you say the stroke descriptions. To help students visualize the letter, model **d** in the air. Have students echo the stroke descriptions as they write **d** in the air with you. Ask questions such as these:
Where does **d** begin? (*just below the midline*)
Where does **d** end? (*at the midline*)
How does **d** begin? (*with a downcurve*)
How does **d** end? (*with an undercurve*)

EVALUATE

To help students evaluate their writing, ask questions such as these:
Does your first undercurve end at the headline?
Does your **d** end at the midline? (visual, auditory)

CORRECTIVE STRATEGY

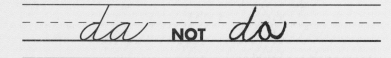
da NOT *do*

The undercurve to downcurve joining becomes a doublecurve.

Name

Write.

di da du dr id

drips paid sad

draw said rid

dad slid dirt

Write your own words.

EVALUATE Circle your best letter. Circle your best joining. Circle your best word.
Copyright © Zaner-Bloser, Inc.   **PRACTICE MASTER 13**

PRACTICE MASTER 13

31

**Downcurve
Undercurve
Slant
Loop forward,
    undercurve**

PRACTICE

Let students use laminated writing cards or slates to practice writing the letter.

COACHING HINT

To stress correct joining strokes, ask the students to write any word in cursive on the chalkboard and to use colored chalk to highlight the joining strokes. (visual)

Name _____

Write.

q q q q q q q

q q q q q q q

qu squ qua qui

quit squirts

squirt quits

quart quarts

Write your own words.

EVALUATE Circle your best letter. Circle your best joining. Circle your best word.
PRACTICE MASTER 14   Copyright © Zaner-Bloser, Inc.

PRACTICE MASTER 14

---

a quintet of quick quails
a quintet of quick quails

Trace and write.

q q   *q q q q q*

Write *q*.

q q q q q q q

Join *q* and other letters.

qu squ qua qui

Circle your best *q*.

Write words with *q*.

quart quits squirt

32

MODEL THE WRITING

Write **q** on guidelines as you say the stroke descriptions. To help students visualize the letter, have them write **q** in the air with you.
Ask questions such as these:
How does **q** begin? *(with a downcurve)*
How does **q** end? *(with an undercurve)*
Where does the loop in **q** close? *(at the baseline)*

EVALUATE

q q q

To help students evaluate their writing, ask questions such as these:
Does your **q** have correct slant?
Does your loop close at the baseline?
Does your loop fill the descender space? (visual, auditory)

CORRECTIVE STRATEGY

q **NOT** *q*

Close the loop at the baseline.

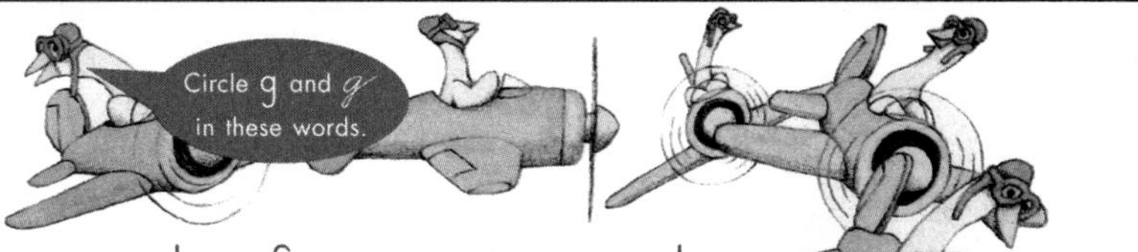

Circle g and *g* in these words.

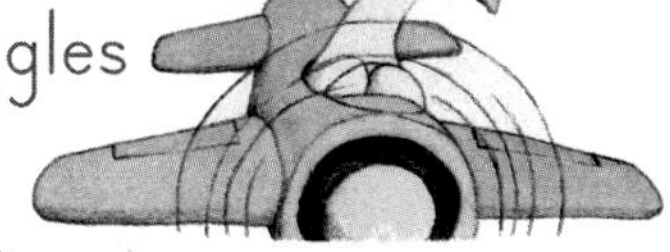

a gaggle of geese in goggles

a gaggle of geese in goggles

Trace and write.

g *g*   *g g g g g*

Write *g*.

g g g g g g g g

Join *g* and other letters.

ga   gi   gu   gr   ag

Write words with *g*.

grip   guitar   dug

Circle your best *g*.

33

MODEL THE WRITING

Write **g** on guidelines as you say the stroke descriptions. Have students echo the stroke descriptions as they write **g** in the air with you. Ask questions such as these:

How does **g** differ from **q**? *(The letter **g** loops back and ends with an overcurve; **q** loops forward and ends with an undercurve.)*

Where does the loop in **g** close? *(at the baseline)*

EVALUATE

g   g

To help students evaluate their writing, ask questions such as these:

Is your letter closed at the top?

Does your loop close at the baseline? (visual, auditory)

CORRECTIVE STRATEGY

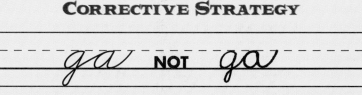

ga   **NOT**   *ga*

In the overcurve to downcurve joining, the overcurve ends at the beginning of the downcurve.

---

g²

Downcurve
Undercurve
Slant
Loop back, overcurve

PRACTICE

Let students use laminated writing cards or slates to practice writing the letter.

WRITE AWAY

Challenge students to use some of these letters (**i, t, u, w, r, s, p, j, a, c, d, q, g**) to form new words by changing one letter in each of these words: *part, star, paws, drag,* and *trip*. Encourage students to write in both cursive and manuscript forms.

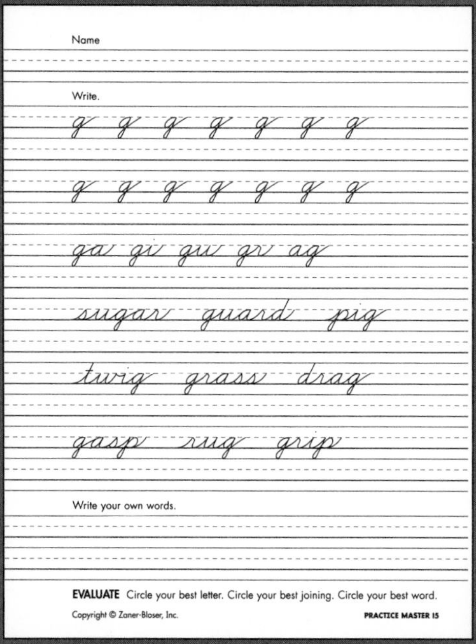

Name

Write.

g g g g g g

g g g g g g

ga gi gu gr ag

sugar guard pig

twig grass drag

gasp rug grip

Write your own words.

EVALUATE Circle your best letter. Circle your best joining. Circle your best word.

Copyright © Zaner-Bloser, Inc.   **PRACTICE MASTER 15**

PRACTICE MASTER 15

Downcurve
Undercurve
Checkstroke

PRACTICE
Let students use laminated writing cards or slates to practice writing the letter.

COACHING HINT
Correct body position is important. Encourage students to sit comfortably erect, with their feet flat on the floor and their hips touching the back of the chair. Both arms rest on the desk. The elbows are off the desk. Tell students they will be able to write more easily and for a longer period of time if they sit in a good writing position.

PRACTICE MASTER 16

34

---

ostriches in an opera
ostriches in an opera

Circle **o** and *o* in these words.

Trace and write.
o o o

Circle your best *o*.

Write *o*.
o   o   o   o   o   o

Join *o* and other letters.
oo oi oa ou ot

Write words with *o*.
post soap stood

across   curious

34

MODEL THE WRITING
Write **o** on guidelines as you say the stroke descriptions. To help students visualize the letter, model **o** in the air. Have students echo the stroke descriptions as they write **o** in the air with you. Ask questions such as these:
Where does **o** begin? *(just below the midline)*
Where does **o** end? *(at the midline)*

EVALUATE
o   o   o

To help students evaluate their writing, ask questions such as these:
Does your **o** begin below the midline?
Is your oval closed?
Does your checkstroke end at the midline? (visual, auditory)

CORRECTIVE STRATEGY
oa **NOT** *oa*

The checkstroke to downcurve joining swings much wider than the checkstroke to undercurve joining because of the downcurve.

Review

Write these words.

carrot   potato   toast

cat   quit   dog   cow

Write these phrases.

two proud actors

Circle your best word.

coast to coast

35

EVALUATE

To help students evaluate their writing, ask questions such as these:
Are your downcurve letters written correctly?
Are your checkstroke joinings written correctly?
Are the size and shape of your letters satisfactory? (visual, auditory)

REFOCUS

Review the letters **a**, **c**, **d**, **q**, **g**, and **o** by writing them on the chalkboard and saying the stroke descriptions with students. Ask a volunteer to demonstrate the correct formation of each letter. Have volunteers give the class clues that describe one of these letters, for example:

• This letter has a loop forward descender. *(q)*
• This letter touches the headline. *(d)*
• This letter ends with a checkstroke. *(o)*

Challenge the other students to identify the letter described. Encourage the volunteers to use correct terms in their clues.

COACHING HINT

Remind students that a little more space is needed before a word that begins with a downcurve letter (**a**, **c**, **d**, **g**, **o**, and **q**). Write on the chalkboard a sentence such as *An alligator gave the ducks quite a scare.* Use colored chalk to indicate the space needed. (visual)

WRITE AWAY

Ask students to make up a name for an all-animal basketball team. Then ask them to write the name of their team and to list the animal members and the positions they play. Participate by telling your own animal team name and the animal that plays each position.

35

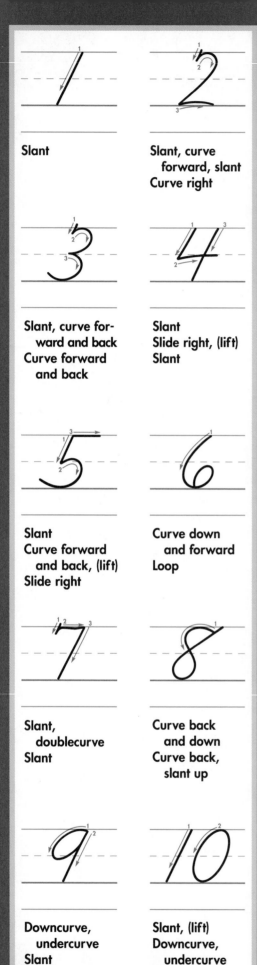

Slant

**Slant, curve
forward, slant
Curve right**

**Slant, curve for-
ward and back
Curve forward
and back**

**Slant
Slide right, (lift)
Slant**

**Slant
Curve forward
and back, (lift)
Slide right**

**Curve down
and forward
Loop**

**Slant,
doublecurve
Slant**

**Curve back
and down
Curve back,
slant up**

**Downcurve,
undercurve
Slant**

**Slant, (lift)
Downcurve,
undercurve**

Numerals

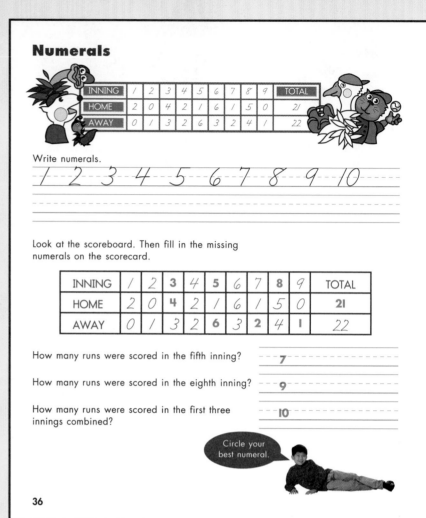

Write numerals.

$\overline{1 \quad 2 \quad 3 \quad 4 \quad 5 \quad 6 \quad 7 \quad 8 \quad 9 \quad 10}$

Look at the scoreboard. Then fill in the missing
numerals on the scorecard.

INNING	1	2	3	4	5	6	7	8	9	TOTAL
HOME	2	0	4	2	1	6	1	5	0	21
AWAY	0	1	3	2	6	3	2	4	1	22

How many runs were scored in the fifth inning? _____ 7

How many runs were scored in the eighth inning? _____ 9

How many runs were scored in the first three
innings combined? _____ 10

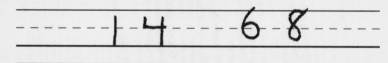

Circle your
best numeral.

36

MODEL THE WRITING

Write the numerals on guidelines as you say the stroke descriptions.
To help students visualize each numeral, model it in the air. Have stu-
dents say the stroke descriptions as they write each numeral in the air
with you. Ask questions such as these:
Where does the numeral **1** begin? *(at the headline)*
What stroke begins the numerals **2** and **3**? *(short slant)*
What is the last stroke in the numeral **5**? *(slide right)*
Where does the numeral **8** begin? *(just below the headline)*

EVALUATE

$\overline{1 \quad 4 \quad 6 \quad 8}$

To help students evaluate their writing, ask questions such as these:
Do your numerals touch the headline?
Do your numerals rest on the baseline? (visual, auditory)

a band of noisy nightingales
a band of noisy nightingales

n *n*

Trace and write.

n n

Circle n and *n* in these words.

Write *n*.

n n n n n

Join *n* and other letters.

na ni ong ing

Circle your best *n*.

Write words with *n*.

narrow again

song stopping

37

Overcurve, slant
Overcurve, slant
Undercurve

PRACTICE
Let students use laminated writing cards or slates to practice writing the letter.

COACHING HINT
Writing rate will increase as students begin to move the writing hand more freely. Have students practice writing letters and words in large size with crayon on folded newsprint to overcome finger motion. (kinesthetic)

MODEL THE WRITING
Write **n** on guidelines as you say the stroke descriptions. Have students echo the stroke descriptions as they write **n** in the air with you. Ask questions such as these:
How does **n** begin? *(with an overcurve)*
How does **n** end? *(with an undercurve)*
How many overcurves are in **n**? *(two)*
How many slant strokes are in **n**? *(two)*

EVALUATE

n n n

To help students evaluate their writing, ask questions such as these:
Are your overcurves round?
Do your overcurves touch the midline?
Are your slant strokes pulled toward the baseline? (visual, auditory)

CORRECTIVE STRATEGY

n **NOT** *n*

Make sure there is enough space between the overcurves.

Name

Write.

n n n n n n n

n n n n n n n

na ni no nt nn ing

now onion ground

running point turn

downtown join

Write your own words.

EVALUATE Circle your best letter. Circle your best joining. Circle your best word.
Copyright © Zaner-Bloser, Inc.   **PRACTICE MASTER 17**

PRACTICE MASTER 17

Overcurve, slant
Overcurve, slant
Overcurve, slant
Undercurve

PRACTICE

Let students use laminated writing cards or slates to practice writing the letter.

COACHING HINT: LEFT-HANDED WRITERS

Right-handed teachers will better understand the stroke, vision, and posture of the left-handed student if they practice the left-handed position themselves. The Zaner-Bloser Writing Frame can help students achieve correct hand position, because the hand holding the pencil and resting over the frame automatically settles into the correct position.

Name

Write.

m m m m m m m

m m m m m m m

mi mo mm mu vm

autumn tomato warm

moon arm mosquito

mountain coming

Write your own words.

EVALUATE Circle your best letter. Circle your best joining. Circle your best word.
PRACTICE MASTER 18   Copyright © Zaner-Bloser, Inc.

PRACTICE MASTER 18

38

Circle m and *m* in these words.

monkeys making marshmallows
monkeys making marshmallows

m *m*

Trace and write.

m m m m

Write *m*.

m m m m m m

Join *m* and other letters.

mi ma mm oom um

Circle your best *m*.

Write words with *m*.

mind   map   room

38

MODEL THE WRITING

Write **m** on guidelines as you say the stroke descriptions. To help students visualize the letter, model **m** in the air. Have students echo the stroke descriptions as they write **m** in the air with you. Ask questions such as these:
How many overcurves are in **m**? *(three)*
How many slant strokes are in **m**? *(three)*
How many times does **m** touch the midline? *(four)*

EVALUATE

m   m

To help students evaluate their writing, ask questions such as these:
Is there enough space between your overcurves?
Does your **m** rest on the baseline? (visual, auditory)

CORRECTIVE STRATEGY

mm   **NOT**   *mm*

The undercurve to overcurve joining becomes a doublecurve. The doublecurve becomes a part of the following letter.

Circle **x** and *x* in these words.

foxes fixing a taxi
foxes fixing a taxi

Trace and write.

x *x*   *x x x x*

Write *x*.

x x x x x x x

Join *x* and other letters.

xa xi ax ix ixt

Write words with *x*.

mixing taxi ox

Circle your best *x*.

39

MODEL THE WRITING

Write **x** on guidelines as you say the stroke descriptions. Model **x** in the air. Have students echo the stroke descriptions as they write **x** in the air with you. Ask questions such as these:

How does **x** begin? *(with an overcurve)*
Where does the overcurve end? *(at the midline)*
Where does the last slant stroke begin? *(at the midline)*
Where does the last slant stroke end? *(at the baseline)*

EVALUATE

x   x

To help students evaluate their writing, ask questions such as these:
Does your **x** have a good overcurve?
Is your **x** crossed in the middle of the first slant stroke? (visual, auditory)

CORRECTIVE STRATEGY

x **NOT** *x*

After writing the overcurve, be sure to slant left toward the baseline.

Overcurve, slant
Undercurve, (lift)
Slant

PRACTICE

Let students use laminated writing cards or slates to practice writing the letter.

WRITE AWAY

Challenge students to form real words by using the letters **i, t, u, w, r, s, p, j, a, c, d, q, g, o, n, m,** and **x** to fill in the blanks of these words.

s__t	groa__	__ow	__ax
s__air	pu__	h__t	p__t
__ar	ad__	twi__	j__in
__ix	__uit	ta__i	__op
mo__n			

mo_o_n

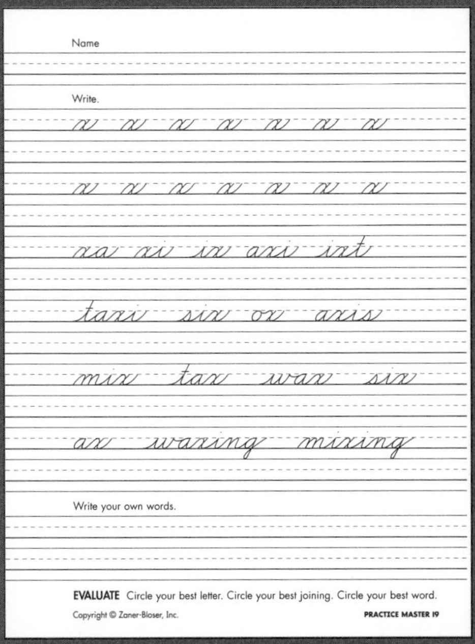

Name

Write.

x x x x x x x

x x x x x x x

xa xi ix axi ixt

taxi six ox axis

mix tax wax six

ox waxing mixing

Write your own words.

EVALUATE Circle your best letter. Circle your best joining. Circle your best word.
Copyright © Zaner-Bloser, Inc.   **PRACTICE MASTER 19**

PRACTICE MASTER 19

39

Overcurve, slant
Undercurve
Slant
Loop back, overcurve

PRACTICE
Let students use laminated writing cards or slates to practice writing the letter.

COACHING HINT
Give half the students manuscript letter cards and the other half the corresponding cursive letter cards. On a signal, have them scramble to locate their partners. Repeat several times to reinforce identification of the cursive letters. (visual, kinesthetic)

PRACTICE MASTER 20

40

yaks playing with yo-yos
yaks playing with yo-yos

Circle y and *y* in these words.

Trace and write.

_y y y_

Write _y_.

_y y y y y_

Join _y_ and other letters.

_ya yo ys ay oy_

Circle your best _y_.

Write words with _y_.

yard   carry

yours   says

40

MODEL THE WRITING
Write **y** on guidelines as you say the stroke descriptions. To help students visualize the letter, model **y** in the air. Have students echo the stroke descriptions as they write **y** in the air with you. Ask questions such as these:
How does **y** end? *(with an overcurve)*
How many overcurves are in **y**? *(two)*

EVALUATE

_y   y   y_

To help students evaluate their writing, ask questions such as these:
Does your loop close at the baseline?
Are your slant strokes pulled correctly toward the baseline?
Does your **y** end with an overcurve at the midline? (visual, auditory)

CORRECTIVE STRATEGY

_y_ **NOT** _y_

Be sure the overcurve ending crosses the slant stroke at the baseline.

zebras zipping zippers
zebras zipping zippers

Trace and write.

Z *Z*

Circle Z and *z* in these words.

Write *z*.

Join *z* and other letters.

zi zo zy az iz

Circle your best *z*

Write words with *z*.

dizzy quiz jazz

zooms zigzag

41

Overcurve, slant
Overcurve
Curve down
Loop, overcurve

maj   og   tuiq
wap   praw   zuiq
rodcto   orrotomw

MODEL THE WRITING
Write **z** on guidelines as you say the stroke descriptions. Have students echo the stroke descriptions as they write **z** in the air with you. Ask questions such as these:
How is the beginning stroke like the ending stroke? *(Both are overcurves.)*
Where does the overcurve ending stop? *(at the midline)*
Where does the loop close? *(at the baseline)*

EVALUATE

Z Z Z

To help students evaluate their writing, ask questions such as these:
Does your loop close at the baseline?
Is your slant stroke pulled toward the baseline?
Does your loop fill the descender space? (visual, auditory)

CORRECTIVE STRATEGY

Z **NOT** *Z*

Close the loop at the baseline.

Name

Write.

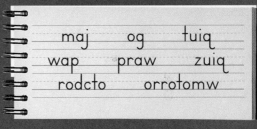

PRACTICE MASTER 21

41

Overcurve, slant
Undercurve
Checkstroke

PRACTICE

Let students use laminated writing cards or slates to practice writing the letter.

COACHING HINT

Most errors in slant can be corrected in one of the following ways:
1. Check paper position.
2. Be sure to pull the slant strokes in the proper direction.
3. Remember to shift the paper as the writing progresses across the line.

Name

Write.

v v v v v v v

v v v v v v v

va vi vo av iv vy

vow visit avoid

van giving waving

victory dividing

Write your own words.

EVALUATE Circle your best letter. Circle your best joining. Circle your best word.
PRACTICE MASTER 22   Copyright © Zaner-Bloser, Inc.

PRACTICE MASTER 22

42

Circle V and *v* in these words.

vultures in vests playing volleyball
vultures in vests playing volleyball

Trace and write.

V *v*   *v v v v*

Write *v*.

v v v v v v v

Join *v* and other letters.

va vi vo av iv vy

Write words with *v*.   Circle your best *v*.

vacation   visiting

42

MODEL THE WRITING

Write **v** on guidelines as you say the stroke descriptions. To help students visualize the letter, model **v** in the air. Have students echo the stroke descriptions as they write **v** in the air with you. Ask questions such as these:
How does **v** end? *(with a checkstroke)*
What strokes are in **v**? *(overcurve, slant, undercurve, checkstroke)*

EVALUATE

v   v   v

To help students evaluate their writing, ask questions such as these:
Does your **v** end with a checkstroke?
Does your **v** have a good slant stroke?
Is your **v** about the same width as the model? (visual, auditory)

CORRECTIVE STRATEGY

v **NOT** *v*

The overcurve stroke curves up and over.

Review

n   m   x   y   z   v

Write these words.

morning   noon   gravy

zooming   mix

Write these phrases.

sixty moving vans

Circle your best word.

six amazing toys

43

REFOCUS

Review the letters **n, m, x, y, z,** and **v**. Ask a volunteer to demonstrate the correct formation of each letter on the chalkboard. Encourage the student to describe the strokes used. Ask each student to write these letters on six cards or pieces of paper. Have students hold up a card that fits each of the following descriptions:

- This letter has no descender. (*n, m, x, v*)
- This letter begins at the baseline. (*n, m, x, y, z, v*)
- This letter has a lift. (*x*)
- This letter crosses itself at the baseline. (*y, z*)
- This letter uses an undercurve to join with the next letter. (*n, m, x*)

COACHING HINT

On the chalkboard, demonstrate the letters with descenders. Have students trace the descender with colored chalk to highlight its shape and size. (kinesthetic, visual)

EVALUATE

To help students evaluate their writing, ask questions such as these:
Are your letters formed correctly?
Are your beginning overcurves rounded? (visual, auditory)

WRITE AWAY

Ask students to write the name of an animal they like and a short explanation of why they like it. Participate by telling the name of an animal you like and why you like it.

MANUSCRIPT MAINTENANCE: SLANT

Before students begin, remind them that manuscript writing is straight up and down. Demonstrate correct paper position and emphasize the direction in which to pull the strokes in order to make lines that are vertical.

COACHING HINT

Demonstrate the placement of lightly drawn parallel vertical lines over manuscript letters as a check of good vertical quality. (visual)

WRITE AWAY

Ask students to use their best manuscript to write and illustrate a movie title about animals. Participate by naming a few movies in which animals play a prominent role.

Manuscript Maintenance: Word Search

Find the animal names in the Word Search. The words may go across or down. Then write them using your best uppercase manuscript.

A	C	S	J	F	D
C	A	P	A	X	J
R	T	I	G	E	R
D	O	G	U	Y	O
F	O	X	A	A	Z
S	T	O	R	K	Q

STORK JAGUAR CAT FOX TIGER YAK PIG DOG

ACROSS	DOWN
TIGER	CAT
DOG	PIG
FOX	JAGUAR
STORK	YAK

EVALUATE

To help students evaluate their writing, ask questions such as these:
Do your letters with pull down straight strokes stand up straight?
Are your slant right strokes slanted correctly?
Are your slant left strokes slanted correctly? (visual, auditory)

MAINTAINING MANUSCRIPT

To emphasize the need for manuscript, discuss situations that require manuscript writing. If possible, provide samples of job applications, subscription cards, test forms, tax returns, and bank forms as examples of the need for manuscript writing. Allow students to practice filling out a form requiring name, address, age, and phone number. Discuss potential problems with these forms if the manuscript is illegible, and role-play such situations.

electric eels on an escalator
electric eels on an escalator

Trace and write.

e ℓ ℓ

Circle e and *e* in these words.

Write *e*.

ℓ ℓ ℓ ℓ ℓ

Join *e* and other letters.

ea ee en ew ie

Write words with *e*.

enjoy east

new everyone

Circle your best *e*.

45

MODEL THE WRITING

Write **e** on guidelines as you say the stroke descriptions. To help students visualize the letter, model **e** in the air. Have students echo the stroke descriptions as they write **e** in the air with you. Ask questions such as these:

How does **e** begin? *(with an undercurve)*
What size letter is **e**? *(short)*

EVALUATE

ℓ ℓ ℓ

To help students evaluate their writing, ask questions such as these:
Are your lines not too light or too dark?
Does your **e** have a good loop?
Does your **e** end at the midline? (visual, auditory)

CORRECTIVE STRATEGY

ℓ **NOT** ℓ

Be sure there is a loop in the letter.

ℓ

Undercurve
Loop back, slant
Undercurve

PRACTICE
Let students use laminated writing cards or slates to practice writing the letter.

COACHING HINT
Keep a record of the letters with which students are having problems. Give students writing exercises such as word lists and tongue twisters that will give them practice with these letters. (visual)

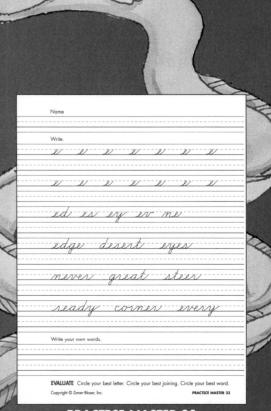

Name

Write.

ℓ ℓ ℓ ℓ ℓ ℓ ℓ

ℓ ℓ ℓ ℓ ℓ ℓ ℓ

ed es ey ew me

edge desert eyes

never great steer

ready corner every

Write your own words.

EVALUATE Circle your best letter. Circle your best joining. Circle your best word.
Copyright © Zaner-Bloser, Inc.   PRACTICE MASTER 23

PRACTICE MASTER 23

**Undercurve
Loop back, slant
Undercurve**

PRACTICE
Let students use laminated writing cards or slates to practice writing the letter.

COACHING HINT
Continue to use the chalkboard for teaching the basic strokes, letters, joinings, and numerals. Students having motor-skill difficulty when they write on lined paper may benefit from the increased spacing the chalkboard provides. Since erasing is easy, identification and correction of errors becomes a simpler task. (kinesthetic, visual)

PRACTICE MASTER 24

46

Circle l and ℓ in these words.

llamas logrolling on a lake
llamas logrolling on a lake

Trace and write.

ℓ ℓ ℓ ℓ ℓ ℓ

Write ℓ.

ℓ ℓ ℓ ℓ ℓ ℓ ℓ

Join ℓ and other letters.

la le lo al ly ll

Write words with ℓ.

lovely   always   list

Circle your best ℓ.

46

MODEL THE WRITING
Write l on guidelines as you say the stroke descriptions. Model l in the air. Have students echo the stroke descriptions as they write l in the air with you. Ask questions such as these:
How are **e** and **l** different? *(The letter **e** is short; **l** is tall.)*
Where does the loop close in **l**? *(near the midline)*
What strokes are in both **e** and **l**? *(undercurve, loop back, slant, undercurve)*

EVALUATE

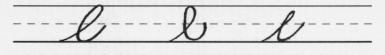

To help students evaluate their writing, ask questions such as these:
Does your loop close near the midline?
Is your slant stroke pulled toward the baseline?
Does your l touch the headline? (visual, auditory)

CORRECTIVE STRATEGY

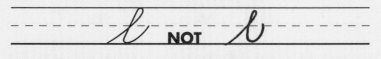

ℓ **NOT** ℓ

Pull the slant stroke straight toward the midsection (right-handers) or toward the left elbow (left-handers).

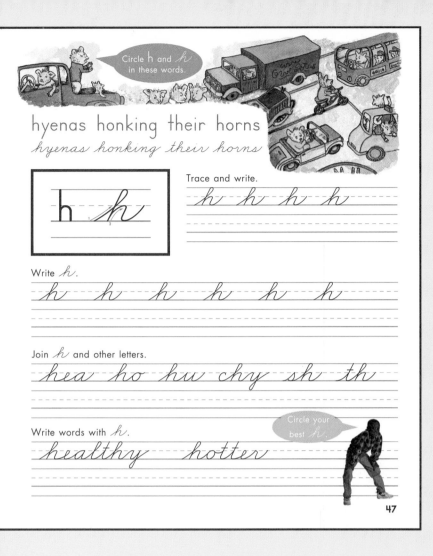

Circle h and *h* in these words.

hyenas honking their horns
hyenas honking their horns

Trace and write.

h h h h

Write *h*.

h h h h h h

Join *h* and other letters.

hea ho hu chy sh th

Write words with *h*.

healthy   hotter

Circle your best *h*.

47

Undercurve
Loop back, slant
Overcurve, slant
Undercurve

PRACTICE

Let students use laminated writing cards or slates to practice writing the letter.

COACHING HINT

On the chalkboard, write a line of lowercase letters with several obvious errors. Ask students to come to the chalkboard to locate, identify, and correct the errors. (visual, kinesthetic)

MODEL THE WRITING

Write **h** on guidelines as you say the stroke descriptions. To help students visualize the letter, model **h** in the air. Have students echo the stroke descriptions as they write **h** in the air with you. Ask questions such as these:
What stroke follows the first slant? *(overcurve)*
How does **h** end? *(with an undercurve)*

EVALUATE

h   h   h

To help students evaluate their writing, ask questions such as these:
Is your **h** about the same width as the model?
Does your loop close near the midline?
Does your overcurve touch the midline? (visual, auditory)

CORRECTIVE STRATEGY

h   NOT   *h*

Close the loop near the midline and keep slant strokes parallel.

Name

Write.

h h h h h h h

h h h h h h h

ght ha hy wh thr

might haircut rhyme

throw which having

earth hundred shed

Write your own words.

EVALUATE Circle your best letter. Circle your best joining. Circle your best word.
Copyright © Zaner-Bloser, Inc.   **PRACTICE MASTER 25**

PRACTICE MASTER 25

Undercurve
Loop back, slant
Overcurve, curve
forward, curve under
Slant right, undercurve

PRACTICE

Let students use laminated writing cards or slates to practice writing the letter.

COACHING HINT

Have students form letters and joinings in a thin layer of finger paint spread on aluminum foil. (kinesthetic)

PRACTICE MASTER 26

48

---

kangaroos in kilts flying kites
kangaroos in kilts flying kites

Trace and write.

k k

Write *k*.

k k k k

Join *k* and other letters.

ke kn ka ck

Write words with *k*.

kind knew desk

quick kept joke

Circle k and *k* in these words.

Circle your best *k*.

48

MODEL THE WRITING

Write **k** on guidelines as you say the stroke descriptions. To help students visualize the letter, model **k** in the air. Have students echo the stroke descriptions as they write **k** in the air with you. Ask questions such as these:
How are **h** and **k** alike? *(Both begin and end with an undercurve; both have a loop that closes near the midline.)*
How many pauses are in **k**? *(two)*

EVALUATE

k   k

To help students evaluate their writing, ask questions such as these:
Is your **k** about the same width as the model?
Does your loop close near the midline? (visual, auditory)

CORRECTIVE STRATEGY

k   **NOT**   *k*

The curve under stroke is followed by a pause, slant right, and undercurve.

a flamingo family pulling taffy
a flamingo family pulling taffy

Circle f and *f* in these words.

Trace and write.

f f

Write *f*.

f f f f f

Join *f* and other letters.

fa fi fo fl ffy

Write words with *f*.

family   forest

half   foxes

Circle your best *f*

49

Undercurve
Loop back, slant
Loop forward
Undercurve

PRACTICE
Let students use laminated writing cards or slates to practice writing the letter.

COACHING HINT
Holding the writing instrument correctly has an obvious effect on handwriting quality. Students having difficulty with the conventional method of holding the writing instrument may wish to try the alternate method of placing the pen or pencil between the first and second fingers. (kinesthetic)

MODEL THE WRITING
Write **f** on guidelines as you say the stroke descriptions. To help students visualize the letter, model **f** in the air. Have students echo the stroke descriptions as they write **f** in the air with you. Ask questions such as these:
How does **f** begin and end? *(with an undercurve)*
Where does the upper loop close? *(near the midline)*

EVALUATE

f   f   f

To help students evaluate their writing, ask questions such as these:
Does your **f** begin and end with an undercurve?
Does your upper loop close near the midline?
Does your lower loop close at the baseline? (visual, auditory)

CORRECTIVE STRATEGY

f **NOT** *f*

Close the lower loop at the baseline.

Name

Write.

f f f f f f

f f f f f f

fe foo fr ffy lf

feather foot free

taffy calf fight

fair few yourself

Write your own words.

EVALUATE Circle your best letter. Circle your best joining. Circle your best word.
Copyright © Zaner-Bloser, Inc.   **PRACTICE MASTER 27**

PRACTICE MASTER 27

Undercurve
Loop back, slant
Undercurve
Checkstroke

PRACTICE

Let students use laminated writing cards or slates to practice writing the letter.

WRITE AWAY

Challenge students to write as many three-letter words as they can using the 26 lowercase letters. You may want to set a time limit. If students are having difficulty, write all 26 letters on the chalkboard.

PRACTICE MASTER 28

Circle b and *b* in these words.

baboons blowing bubbles
baboons blowing bubbles

Trace and write.

b b b b b

Write *b*.

b b b b b b b

Join *b* and other letters.

ba bea by bo ub

Write words with *b*.

because bought

Circle your best *b*.

MODEL THE WRITING

Write **b** on guidelines as you say the stroke descriptions. To help students visualize the letter, model **b** in the air. Have students echo the stroke descriptions as they write **b** in the air with you. Ask questions such as these:
Where does the loop close in **b**? *(near the midline)*
How does **b** differ from **l**? *(The letter **b** ends with a checkstroke.)*

EVALUATE

b   b   b

To help students evaluate their writing, ask questions such as these:
Does your loop close near the midline?
Does your second undercurve end at the midline?
Does your checkstroke end at the midline? (visual, auditory)

CORRECTIVE STRATEGY

be **NOT** *be*

In the checkstroke to undercurve joining, deepen the checkstroke a little before swinging into the undercurve of the next letter.

Review

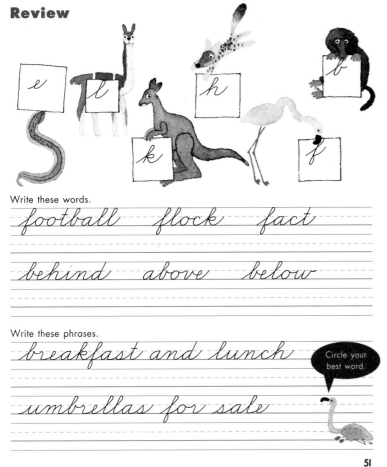

Write these words.

football   flock   fact

behind   above   below

Write these phrases.

breakfast and lunch

Circle your best word.

umbrellas for sale

51

REFOCUS
Review the letters **e**, **l**, **h**, **k**, **f**, and **b** by writing them on the chalkboard as you say the stroke descriptions. Review the undercurve to undercurve and checkstroke to undercurve joinings. Have volunteers write the following combinations on the chalkboard:

le	**hi**	**lk**	**be**
bi	**fr**	**es**	**bl**

Encourage students to describe both the strokes and the joinings as they form them, using the correct terms.

WRITE AWAY
Ask students to choose one of the animals shown at the top of page 51 and to write a description of what its lunch box might contain. Participate by describing the possible contents of an animal's lunch box.

EVALUATE
To help students evaluate their writing, ask questions such as these:
Do all your letters end at the midline?
Do your tall letters touch the headline?
Does your **b** end with a checkstroke? (visual, auditory)

In Other Words

Students can use these pages to practice writing cursive words in other languages. Remind students to include any accent marks in the words they are writing.

If there are students who read Spanish or French, ask them to read aloud the words in those languages and to help the other students pronounce them correctly. If there are students who know words in languages other than English, Spanish, or French, invite them to write the words in the blank grids provided for that purpose.

COACHING HINT

Keep a record of the lowercase letters that give students trouble. Give them writing exercises such as word lists and tongue twisters to provide practice with these letters.

Practice Masters 72–93 provide additional practice in writing in Spanish.

In Other Words

English
cap

English
ball

French
casquette

French
balle

Spanish
gorro

Spanish
pelota

Other Languages

Other Languages

52

French

casquette (kask EHT)
balle (BAL)
pomme (PAWM)
pastèque (pas THEK)

Spanish

pelota (peh LOH tah)
gorro (GOH *rroh*)*
manzana (mahn ZAH nah)
sandía (sahn DEE ah)

*trilled or rolled *r* used in Spanish pronunciations

English

apple

French

pomme

Spanish

manzana

Other Languages

English

watermelon

French

pastèque

Spanish

sandía

Other Languages

WRITE AWAY
Provide students with English-Spanish and English-French dictionaries. Challenge students to find and write the same word in two of the languages (or in any language they choose).

EVALUATE

To help students evaluate their writing, ask questions such as these:
Do your tall letters touch the headline?
Do your short letters touch the midline?
Do your letters with descenders extend below the baseline? (visual, auditory)

Tell students they now have studied and written all the lowercase letterforms. Guide them in a review of these letters with the following activity.

1. The letters **b, e, f, h, i, j, k, l, p, r, s, t, u,** and **w** begin with the _____ stroke. (*undercurve*)

2. The letters **a, c, d, g, o,** and **q** begin with the _____ stroke. (*downcurve*)

3. The letters that begin with the overcurve stroke are_____. (*m, n, x, v, z, y*)

4. The letters **f, g, j, p, q, y,** and **z** have a _____. (*descender*)

5. The letters **b, o, v,** and **w** end with a _____. (*checkstroke*)

Have students review and practice the basic cursive strokes.

54

Review Lowercase Letters

a   b   c   d   e   f   g

n   o   p   q   r   s   t

Write these lowercase letters in cursive.

t w p r

i j s u

c o a g d q

m n x v z y

b k h f e l

Write these words in cursive.

busy _____   porch _____

true _____   giraffe _____

junk _____   maze _____

view _____   queen _____

excited _____   hello _____

54

To help students evaluate their writing, ask questions such as these:
Are your letters formed correctly?
Do your tall letters touch the headline?
Do your short letters touch the midline?
Do your letters with descenders fill the descender space? (visual, auditory)

Certificates of Progress *should be awarded to those students who show notable handwriting progress and Certificates of Excellence to those who progress to the top levels of handwriting ability.*

h i j k l m

u v w x y z

Change the order of the letters to write a new word.

tab foal chin

bat loaf inch

gum rate peal

mug tear pale; leap

Change the first letter to write a new word. **Answers will vary.**

moat fill cast

get pay bell

Circle your best word.

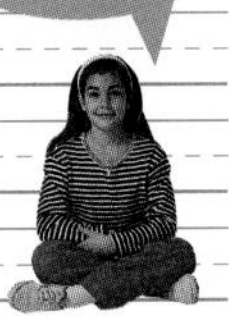

EVALUATE

To help students evaluate their writing, ask questions such as these:
Are your joinings formed correctly?
Do your tall letters touch the headline?
Do your short letters touch the midline?
Do your letters with descenders fill the descender space? (visual, auditory)

COACHING HINT

Put paste or glue on a large letter model and add salt or sand for students to trace. (kinesthetic, visual)

WRITE AWAY

Ask students to write and illustrate a description of a real or an imaginary visit to a farm. Participate by describing your visit to a farm.

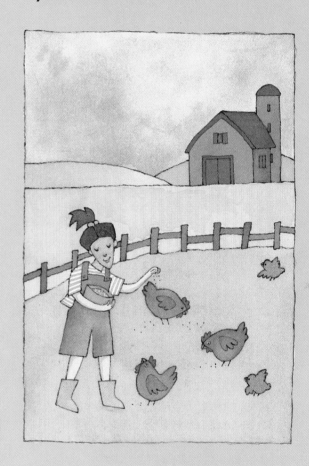

Remind students they have studied and written the lowercase cursive letters grouped according to beginning strokes. Write the cursive lowercase alphabet on the chalkboard and guide students in choosing the letters that complete each category of the chart below:

undercurve ending letters (a, c, d, e, f, h, i, k, l, m, n, p, q, r, s, t, u, x)	undercurve beginning letters (i, t, u, w, r, s, p, j, e, l, h, k, f, b)
overcurve ending letters (g, j, y, z)	downcurve beginning letters (a, c, d, q, g, o)
checkstroke ending letters (b, o, v, w)	overcurve beginning letters (n, m, x, y, z, v)

Tell students that joinings are formed by placing any letter from one column with a letter from the other column. If we choose the letter **a** from the left column and write it with the letter **i** from the right column, we have joined an undercurve-ending letter with an undercurve-beginning letter to form the undercurve-to-undercurve joining **ai**.

Choose several of these joinings and list them on the chalkboard:

undercurve to undercurve
undercurve to downcurve
undercurve to overcurve
overcurve to undercurve
overcurve to downcurve
overcurve to overcurve
checkstroke to undercurve
checkstroke to downcurve
checkstroke to overcurve

Have students choose letter pairs to form examples of each joining, and list their suggestions on the chalkboard with the proper joining label.

Joinings

Write each joining.

li   et   cu   pe

eg   na   rm   dy

ze   gi   yo   ja

gn   zy   br   wi

va   bo   ov   wn

Circle your best joining.

56

Write these words.

often   jumping

yellow   brought

friends   another

cave   xylophone

unable   trick

Circle your best joining in each word.

Put an **x** under a joining that could be better.

57

COACHING HINT
To stress correct joining strokes, ask a volunteer to write any word on the chalkboard. Then have a second volunteer use colored chalk to highlight the joining strokes. (visual)

WRITE AWAY
Have students write and illustrate a story about an endangered animal. Participate by discussing endangered animals.

EVALUATE
To help students evaluate their writing, ask questions such as these:
Which of your joinings are satisfactory?
Which of your joinings need improvement? (visual, auditory)

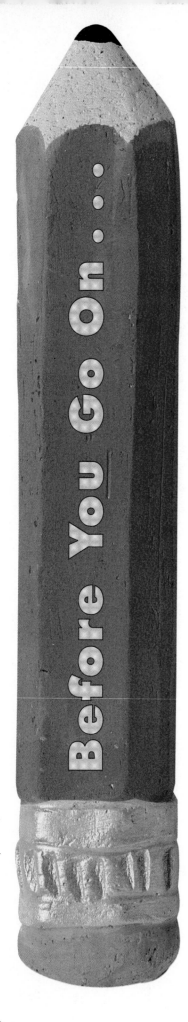

y name is abbit.

What's wrong with this picture?

Writing Uppercase Letters

You use uppercase letters to begin names and sentences. Circle the uppercase letters in your first and last names.

$$\mathcal{A} \; \mathcal{B} \; \mathcal{C} \; \mathcal{D} \; \mathcal{E} \; \mathcal{F} \; \mathcal{G}$$

$$\mathcal{H} \; \mathcal{I} \; \mathcal{J} \; \mathcal{K} \; \mathcal{L} \; \mathcal{M} \; \mathcal{N}$$

$$\mathcal{O} \; \mathcal{P} \; \mathcal{Q} \; \mathcal{R} \; \mathcal{S} \; \mathcal{T} \; \mathcal{U}$$

$$\mathcal{V} \; \mathcal{W} \; \mathcal{X} \; \mathcal{Y} \; \mathcal{Z}$$

In the following pages, you will write uppercase cursive letters in names and sentences. You will pay attention to the size and shape of letters to help make your writing easy to read.

58

UNIT SUMMARY

This page tells students about the content, organization, and focus of the unit. Students are told that uppercase letters begin names and sentences. Then they are introduced to the first two keys to legibility for uppercase letters: size and shape. The lessons that follow emphasize uppercase letter formation and joinings and provide opportunities for writing uppercase letters in different contexts. Students evaluate their work and circle their best uppercase letter in each lesson.

PREVIEW THE UNIT

Preview the unit with students, calling attention to these features:

- letter models in both manuscript and cursive
- cursive letter models with numbered directional arrows
- guidelines for student writing directly beneath handwriting models
- hints about joining uppercase letters to the letter that follows
- brief independent writing activities
- opportunities to evaluate uppercase letter size and shape
- writing activities for manuscript maintenance
- review lessons of uppercase letters grouped by initial stroke

Keys to Legibility: Size and Shape

Help make your writing easy to read.
Pay attention to the size and shape of uppercase letters.

All uppercase letters are tall letters.

𝒜 ℬ 𝒞

𝒥, 𝒴, and 𝒵 are letters with descenders.

𝒥 𝒴 𝒵

Look at the letters below. Circle the green letters that are the correct size and shape.

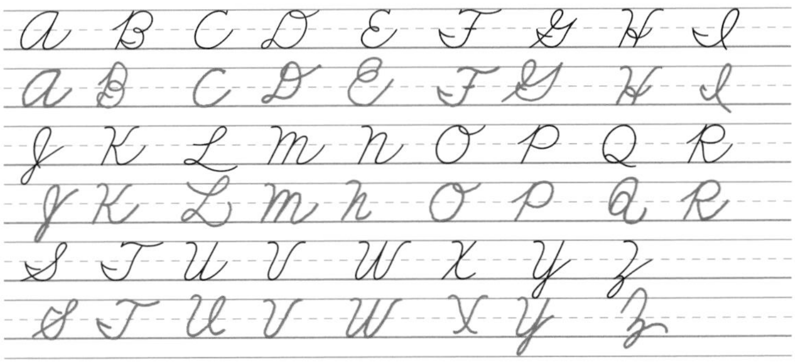

𝒜 ℬ 𝒞 𝒟 ℰ ℱ 𝒢 ℋ �ℐ
𝒜 ℬ 𝒞 𝒟 ℰ ℱ 𝒢 ℋ �ℐ
𝒥 𝒦 ℒ ℳ 𝒩 𝒪 𝒫 𝒬 ℛ
𝒥 𝒦 ℒ ℳ 𝒩 𝒪 𝒫 𝒬 ℛ
𝒮 𝒯 𝒰 𝒱 𝒲 𝒳 𝒴 𝒵
𝒮 𝒯 𝒰 𝒱 𝒲 𝒳 𝒴 𝒵

59

COACHING HINT: SIZE

Demonstrate for students the technique of drawing a horizontal line with a ruler along the tops of letters to show proper size. Have students come to the chalkboard and use colored chalk and a ruler to draw a horizontal line along the top of a group of uppercase letters. Have students practice this technique periodically to evaluate their own letter size in all subject areas. (kinesthetic, visual)

COACHING HINT: SHAPE

Review with students the use of the guidelines for correct letter formation. As you demonstrate on the chalkboard, have students do the following on practice paper:

• Draw over the baseline with a red crayon.

• Draw over the headline and midline with a blue crayon. (kinesthetic, visual, auditory)

KEYS TO LEGIBILITY: SIZE AND SHAPE

Tell students that all uppercase letters are tall letters that touch the headline. Some uppercase letters have descenders.

PRACTICE MASTERS FOR UNIT 3

Letters, 29–54
Stroke Descriptions—English, 66–68
Stroke Descriptions—Spanish, 69–71
Certificates, 57–59
Record of Student's Handwriting Skills, 56
Zaner-Bloser Handwriting Grid, 94

Downcurve
Undercurve
Slant, undercurve

PRACTICE
Let students use laminated writing cards or slates to practice writing the letter.

COACHING HINT
Write each student's name on a self-adhesive ruled name strip. Laminate it if you wish. Place the name strip on the student's desk to serve as a permanent model. (kinesthetic, visual)

PRACTICE MASTER 29

Circle A and *a* in these words.

Anteaters eat ants and termites.
Anteaters eat ants and termites.

Trace and write.

a is joined to the letter that follows. Write words that begin with a.

April August Alaska

Write a sentence that begins with *a*.

An anteater has no teeth.

On Your Own Write a sentence about the month of August.

Circle your best *a*.

MODEL THE WRITING
Write **A** on guidelines as you say the stroke descriptions. To help students visualize the letter, model **A** in the air. Have students echo the stroke descriptions as they write **A** in the air with you. Ask questions such as these:
How many strokes are in **A**? *(four)*
What are they? *(downcurve, undercurve, slant, undercurve)*

EVALUATE

To help students evaluate their writing, ask questions such as these:
Is your **A** closed?
Does your **A** end at the midline?
Is your slant stroke pulled toward the baseline? (visual, auditory)

CORRECTIVE STRATEGY

a **NOT** *a*

Pause before writing the slant stroke.

Coyotes howl at night.

Coyotes howl at night.

Trace and write.

C is joined to the letter that follows. Write words that begin with C.

Canada   Celsius   Craig

Write a sentence that begins with C.

Certain coyotes eat fruit.

On Your Own Write a sentence about Canada.

Circle your best C.

61

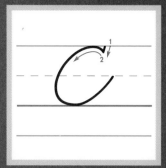

Slant
Downcurve
Undercurve

PRACTICE
Let students use laminated writing cards or slates to practice writing the letter.

WRITE AWAY
Ask students to write a letter they would like to send to a third-grader in China. Encourage students to ask questions that would increase their understanding of another culture. Participate by suggesting questions you would ask of a teacher in China.

MODEL THE WRITING
Write **C** on guidelines as you say the stroke descriptions. To help students visualize the letter, model **C** in the air. Have students echo the stroke descriptions as they write **C** in the air with you. Ask questions such as these:
How does **C** begin? *(with a slant)*
What follows the slant? *(downcurve)*

EVALUATE

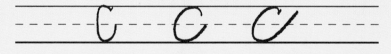

To help students evaluate their writing, ask questions such as these:
Does your **C** have correct slant?
Does your **C** begin with a slant stroke?
Does your **C** end at the midline? (visual, auditory)

CORRECTIVE STRATEGY

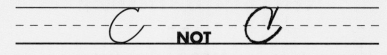

NOT

The first stroke is a short slant that begins at the headline.

Name

Write.

China   Carl   Cyndi

China is on the continent of Asia

Write a sentence that begins with C.

EVALUATE Circle your best C. Circle your best word.
PRACTICE MASTER 30   Copyright © Zaner-Bloser, Inc.

PRACTICE MASTER 30

61

Slant
Downcurve, loop
Downcurve, undercurve

PRACTICE
Let students use laminated writing cards or slates to practice writing the letter.

COACHING HINT
Using card stock or other heavy paper, cut out the parts of a letter (basic strokes) and have the students put them together to form the letter. (kinesthetic)

Name _____

Write.

E E E E E E E

E E E E E E E

Europe   England   Earl

*Emma visited many
places in Europe*

Write a sentence that begins with the word *Every.*

EVALUATE Circle your best *E.* Circle your best word.
Copyright © Zaner-Bloser, Inc.   PRACTICE MASTER 31

PRACTICE MASTER 31

62

Circle **E** and *E* in these words.

Elephants have ivory tusks.
Elephants have ivory tusks.

Trace and write.

E E E E E E E

E is joined to the letter that follows. Write words that begin with *E.*

Earth   Erie   English

Write a sentence that begins with *E.*

Elephants have trunks.

On Your Own Write a sentence about elephants.

Circle your best *E.*

62

MODEL THE WRITING
Write **E** on guidelines as you say the stroke descriptions. To help students visualize the letter, model **E** in the air. Have students echo the stroke descriptions as they write **E** in the air with you. Ask questions such as these:
How many loops are in **E**? *(one)*
Where is it? *(at the midline)*
Where does **E** end? *(at the midline)*

EVALUATE

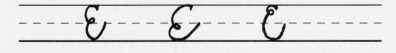

To help students evaluate their writing, ask questions such as these:
Is the slant of your **E** correct?
Is your loop at the midline?
Are your downcurves the correct size? *(visual, auditory)*

CORRECTIVE STRATEGY

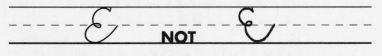

NOT

The bottom downcurve is larger and farther to the left.

Ostriches are the largest birds.

Ostriches are the largest birds.

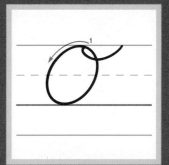

Circle O and *O* in these words.

Trace and write.

O O O O

O is not joined to the letter that follows. Write words that begin with *O*.

October Olympics Oki

Write a sentence that begins with *O*.

Ostriches live in Africa.

On Your Own Write a sentence that begins with *O*.

Circle your best *O*

63

PRACTICE

Let students use laminated writing cards or slates to practice writing the letter.

WRITE AWAY

Ask students to imagine they are members of the United States Olympic Team. Have them write a description of what they would do as members of the team. Participate by describing what you would do.

MODEL THE WRITING

Write **O** on guidelines as you say the stroke descriptions. To help students visualize the letter, model **O** in the air. Have students echo the stroke descriptions as they write **O** in the air with you. Ask questions such as these:

Where does **O** begin? (*just below the headline*)
How many pauses are in **O**? (*none*)

EVALUATE

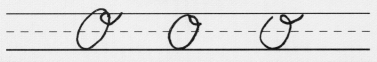

To help students evaluate their writing, ask questions such as these:
Does your **O** begin below the headline?
Does your **O** end at the headline?
Is your **O** closed? (visual, auditory)

CORRECTIVE STRATEGY

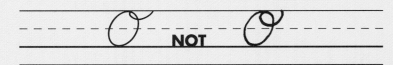

NOT

Dip the loop down slightly, then curve right to end at the headline.

Name

Write.

O O O O O O

O O O O O O

Oklahoma Orlando

Ohio's capital is Columbus.

Write a sentence about the month of October.

EVALUATE Circle your best *O*. Circle your best word.
PRACTICE MASTER 32   Copyright © Zaner-Bloser, Inc.

PRACTICE MASTER 32

63

Review the uppercase letters **A, C, E,** and **O** by asking questions such as these:

Which letters are joined to the letter that follows? *(A, C, E)*

Which letter is not joined to the letter that follows? *(O)*

Ask pairs of students to find four words, one for each of these uppercase letters. Refer them to a class list, name-tags, book titles, a glossary, or any other source of words beginning with uppercase letters. Set a time limit of three to five minutes for the search. Ask each pair of students to write their four words on the chalkboard, describing the strokes and joining techniques.

COACHING HINT

Students who hold the pencil too tightly or do not use the correct position may benefit from the use of the Zaner-Bloser Writing Frame. This teaching aid adapts for either right- or left-hand use and fosters correct hand position and arm movement.

WRITE AWAY

Ask students to choose a mountain range named on page 64 and to write two factual sentences about it or to write a story with that range as a setting. Participate by telling two things about a mountain range of your choice.

Review

Write names of mountain ranges.

Andes   Oeta   Catskill

Elburz   Ozark   Alps

Write these sentences.

Oya saw the Andes.

Circle your best word.

Ed likes the Cascades.

64

EVALUATE

To help students evaluate their writing, ask questions such as these:

Are your downcurve strokes correct in **A, C, E,** and **O**?

Are your **A, C,** and **E** joined properly to the letter that follows? (visual, auditory)

Nightingales migrate to Africa.

Nightingales migrate to Africa.

Circle N and *n* in these words.

Trace and write.

N *n*

n *n* *n* *n* *n*

n is joined to the letter that follows. Write words that begin with *n*.

November Neptune Nat

Write a sentence that begins with *n*.

Not all nightingales sing.

On Your Own Write a sentence about the planet Neptune.

Circle your best *n*.

65

MODEL THE WRITING

Write **N** on guidelines as you say the stroke descriptions. To help students visualize the letter, model **N** in the air. Have students echo the stroke descriptions as they write **N** in the air with you. Ask questions such as these:

How does **N** begin? *(with a curve forward)*
How many slant strokes are in **N**? *(two)*

EVALUATE

To help students evaluate their writing, ask questions such as these:
Are your slant strokes pulled toward the baseline?
Is your overcurve round? (visual, auditory)

CORRECTIVE STRATEGY

n **NOT** *n*

Make sure the overcurve is round.

Curve forward, slant
Overcurve, slant
Undercurve

PRACTICE

Let students use laminated writing cards or slates to practice writing the letter.

WRITE AWAY

Ask students to discuss November events and typical weather conditions. Have them write a paragraph about the month of November.

Name

Write.

n *n* *n* *n* *n* *n*

n *n* *n* *n* *n* *n*

Nancy Nick Nyles

Nellie likes to play soccer.

Write a sentence about a boy named Neil.

EVALUATE Circle your best *n*. Circle your best word.
Copyright © Zaner-Bloser, Inc.   PRACTICE MASTER 33

PRACTICE MASTER 33

Curve forward, slant
Overcurve, slant
Overcurve, slant
Undercurve

PRACTICE

Let students use laminated writing cards or slates to practice writing the letter.

COACHING HINT

To ensure correct paper placement, place the paper at the proper height on the desk for each student and use tape to create a frame on the desk around each corner of the paper. (Do not tape the paper to the desk.) The student will now be able to place the paper in the correct position. (kinesthetic, visual)

Name

Write.

m m m m m m m

m m m m m m m

Mars   Mercury   Mrs.

My teacher's name
is Mr. Moore.

Write a sentence that begins with m.

EVALUATE Circle your best m. Circle your best word.
PRACTICE MASTER 34   Copyright © Zaner-Bloser, Inc.

PRACTICE MASTER 34

Circle M and m
in these words.

Monkeys sleep in trees.
Monkeys sleep in trees.

Trace and write.

M m

m m m m m

m is joined to the letter that follows. Write words that begin with m.

March   May   Monday

Write a sentence that begins with m.

Most monkeys have tails.

On Your Own Write a sentence about Monday.

Circle your best m

66

MODEL THE WRITING

Write **M** on guidelines as you say the stroke descriptions. To help students visualize the letter, model **M** in the air. Have students echo the stroke descriptions as they write **M** in the air with you. Ask questions such as these:
How many slant strokes are in **M**? *(three)*
Where does **M** end? *(at the midline)*

EVALUATE

m   M   M

To help students evaluate their writing, ask questions such as these:
Are your slant strokes pulled toward the baseline?
Does your **M** end at the midline?
Is your second overcurve shorter than your first? (visual, auditory)

CORRECTIVE STRATEGY

m   NOT   m

Pause after the first and second slant strokes.

Kangaroos hop on their hind legs.

Kangaroos hop on their hind legs.

Trace and write.

K K K K K K

$\mathcal{K}$ is joined to the letter that follows. Write words that begin with $\mathcal{K}$.

Kansas Kentucky Kyle

Write a sentence that begins with $\mathcal{K}$.

Kangaroos have big ears.

On Your Own Write a sentence about kangaroos. Circle your best $\mathcal{K}$.

67

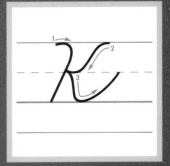

Curve forward, slant,
(lift)
Doublecurve
Curve forward,
undercurve

PRACTICE
Let students use laminated writing cards or slates to practice writing the letter.

WRITE AWAY
Ask students to think of an animal they want to know more about. Have them look up the animal in a children's encyclopedia and read the entry. Tell them to write about the animal and to illustrate their work. Participate by suggesting an animal you would like to know more about.

MODEL THE WRITING
Write **K** on guidelines as you say the stroke descriptions. To help students visualize the letter, model **K** in the air. Have students echo the stroke descriptions as they write **K** in the air with you. Ask questions such as these:
Where is the lift in **K**? *(after the slant)*
What stroke follows the lift? *(doublecurve)*

EVALUATE

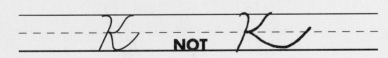

To help students evaluate their writing, ask questions such as these:
Does your **K** rest on the baseline?
Is your **K** about the same width as the model?
Does your **K** end at the midline? (visual, auditory)

CORRECTIVE STRATEGY

K **NOT** *K*

Curve forward before the undercurve ending.

Name

Write.

K K K K K K K

K K K K K K K

Kyle Korea Kansas

Kelly and Kimber are twins

Write a sentence about a girl named Karen.

EVALUATE Circle your best $\mathcal{K}$. Circle your best word.
Copyright © Zaner-Bloser, Inc.   **PRACTICE MASTER 35**

PRACTICE MASTER 35

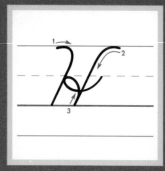

Curve forward, slant,
(lift)
Curve back, slant
Retrace, loop, curve
right

PRACTICE

Let students use laminated writing cards
or slates to practice writing the letter.

COACHING HINT

Provide a small amount of shaving
cream, a drop of tempera paint, and a
paper plate for each student. Direct the
students to mix the shaving cream and
paint with their fingertips and to practice the strokes and letters you call out.
(kinesthetic)

68

Hippos can run as fast as people.

Hippos can run as fast as people.

> Circle H and _H_ in these words.

Trace and write.

H _H_

_H H H H H_

_H_ is joined to the letter that follows. Write words that begin with _H._

Hawaii   Helen   Hiram

Write a sentence that begins with _H._

How heavy is a hippo?

On Your Own Write a sentence about Hawaii.

> Circle your best _H._

68

MODEL THE WRITING

Write **H** on guidelines as you say the stroke descriptions. To help
students visualize the letter, model **H** in the air. Have students echo the
stroke descriptions as they write **H** in the air with you. Ask questions
such as these:
How many loops are in **H**? *(one)*
How many lifts are in **H**? *(one)*
Where does **H** end? *(at the midline)*

EVALUATE

_H   H   H_

To help students evaluate their writing, ask questions such as these:
Is your **H** about the same width as the model?
Does your loop touch the first slant stroke at the midline?
Does your **H** end at the midline? *(visual, auditory)*

CORRECTIVE STRATEGY

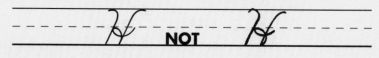

_H_ **NOT** _H_

Retrace before the loop.

Review

Write names of rivers in the United States.

Missouri Kentucky Neosho

Mississippi   Hudson

Write these sentences.

How long is the Neosho?

Meet Ki at the river.

Circle your best word.

69

To help students evaluate their writing, ask questions such as these:
Are the size and shape of your **N, M, K,** and **H** satisfactory?
Are **N, M, K,** and **H** joined properly to the letter that follows? (visual, auditory)

REFOCUS
Review the letters **N, M, K,** and **H** by writing them on the chalkboard as students say the strokes with you. Ask questions such as these:
Which letters are joined to the letter that follows? *(all)*
How do all the letters begin? *(with a curve forward stroke)*

Ask the students whose first, middle, or last names begin with **N, M, K,** and **H** to write their names on the chalkboard.

COACHING HINT: LEFT-HANDED WRITERS
Right-handed teachers can invite a left-handed person to serve as a model. Another teacher, an older student, or a parent could visit the classroom to assist left-handed writers.

WRITE AWAY
Ask students to choose a river named on page 69 and to write two factual sentences about it or to write a story with that river as a setting. Participate by telling two things about a river of your choice.

MANUSCRIPT MAINTENANCE: SIZE

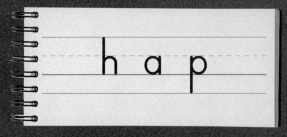

h a p

Manuscript letters of the same size should be the same height. Review with students tall letters (**b, d, f, h, k, l, t,** and all uppercase letters); short letters (**a, c, e, i, m, n, o, r, s, u, v, w, x, z**); and short letters that extend below the baseline (**g, j, p, q, y**).

COACHING HINT

Emphasize the importance of maintaining manuscript writing skills. Provide a wide range of experiences in filling out forms and applications in the classroom. (visual, kinesthetic)

WRITE AWAY

Ask students to use their best manuscript to write and illustrate a magazine ad for Otto, the computerized robot. Participate by reading a few magazine ads aloud to the class.

Manuscript Maintenance: Palindromes

A palindrome is a word, phrase, or sentence that is spelled exactly the same forward and backward.

Write these palindromes in your best manuscript.

wow   pup   eye   did   noon   peep

Bob   Otto   Hannah

Step on no pets.   Was it a cat I saw?

On Your Own Write a palindrome of your own.

EVALUATE

To help students evaluate their writing, ask questions such as these:
Do your short letters touch the midline?
Do your tall letters touch the headline? (visual, auditory)

 MAINTAINING MANUSCRIPT

Use manuscript on the chalkboard for various purposes, especially vocabulary and dictionary study, as well as other work involving word attack skills.

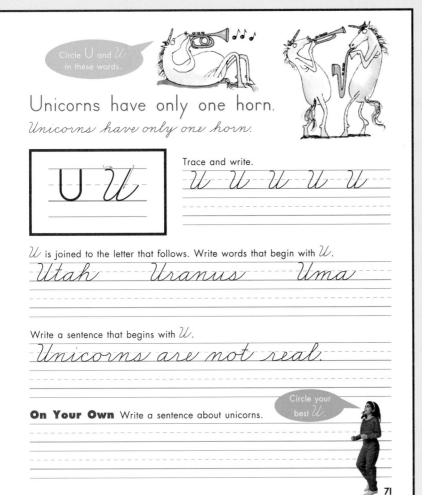

Circle U and *U* in these words.

Unicorns have only one horn.

Unicorns have only one horn.

Trace and write.

U U U U U

U is joined to the letter that follows. Write words that begin with *U.*

Utah   Uranus   Uma

Write a sentence that begins with *U.*

Unicorns are not real.

On Your Own Write a sentence about unicorns.

Circle your best *U.*

71

Curve forward, slant
Undercurve
Slant, undercurve

PRACTICE
Let students use laminated writing cards or slates to practice writing the letter.

WRITE AWAY
Ask students to create an imaginary animal by combining the features of two or more real animals. Have students write a description of their imaginary animal and illustrate it. Participate by describing your own imaginary animal.

MODEL THE WRITING
Write **U** on guidelines as you say the stroke descriptions. To help students visualize the letter, model **U** in the air. Have students echo the stroke descriptions as they write **U** in the air with you. Ask questions such as these:
How many undercurves are in **U**? *(two)*
Where does the first undercurve end? *(at the headline)*
Where does the second undercurve end? *(at the midline)*

EVALUATE

To help students evaluate their writing, ask questions such as these:
Are your slant strokes pulled toward the baseline?
Does your first undercurve end at the headline?
Does your **U** rest on the baseline? (visual, auditory)

CORRECTIVE STRATEGY

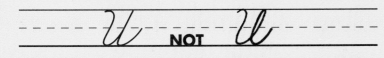

Pause before the second slant stroke.

Name

Write.

U U U U U U U

U U U U U U U

Udine   Umberto   Utica

Uranus is larger
than Neptune.

Write a sentence that begins with *U.*

EVALUATE Circle your best *U.* Circle your best word.
Copyright © Zaner-Bloser, Inc.   **PRACTICE MASTER 37**

PRACTICE MASTER 37

71

Curve forward, slant
Undercurve
Slant
Loop back, overcurve

PRACTICE
Let students use laminated writing cards or slates to practice writing the letter.

COACHING HINT
Holding the pencil too tightly is a common problem that causes a student to tire easily when writing. To overcome this problem, have the student crumple a piece of paper, place it in the palm of the writing hand, and pick up the pencil. This will serve as a reminder not to "squeeze" the pencil. (kinesthetic)

Name

Write.

Yvette Yoli Yuma

Yoko took a trip to New York.

Write a sentence about New York.

EVALUATE Circle your best *y*. Circle your best word.

PRACTICE MASTER 38   Copyright © Zaner-Bloser, Inc.

PRACTICE MASTER 38

72

Circle Y and *y* in these words.

Yaks are good swimmers.
Yaks are good swimmers.

Trace and write.

y is joined to the letter that follows. Write words that begin with *y*.

Yangtze   Yukon   Yves

Write a sentence that begins with *y*.

Yaks have long hair.

On Your Own Write a sentence that begins with *y*.

Circle your best *y*.

72

MODEL THE WRITING
Write **Y** on guidelines as you say the stroke descriptions. To help students visualize the letter, model **Y** in the air. Have students echo the stroke descriptions as they write **Y** in the air with you. Ask questions such as these:
How does **Y** end? *(with an overcurve)*
Where does the loop close? *(at the baseline)*

EVALUATE

To help students evaluate their writing, ask questions such as these:
Is your **Y** about the same size as the model?
Does your **Y** end with an overcurve?
Does your overcurve cross at the baseline? (visual, auditory)

CORRECTIVE STRATEGY

Y **NOT** *Y*

Pause after the undercurve.

Zebras live in Zimbabwe.

Circle Z and z in these words.

Zebras live in Zimbabwe.

Zebras live in Zimbabwe.

Trace and write.

$\mathcal{Z}$ is joined to the letter that follows. Write words that begin with $\mathcal{Z}$.

Zambia   Zurich   Zoe

Write a sentence that begins with $\mathcal{Z}$.

Zebras have stripes.

On Your Own Write a sentence about zebras.

Circle your best Z

73

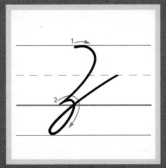

Curve forward, slant
Overcurve, curve down
Loop, overcurve

PRACTICE
Let students use laminated writing cards or slates to practice writing the letter.

WRITE AWAY
Ask students to make up a boy's or girl's name beginning with the letter **Z**. Have them write a brief "biography" of their imaginary person. Participate by describing your own imaginary person with a first initial of **Z**.

MODEL THE WRITING
Write **Z** on guidelines as you say the stroke descriptions. To help students visualize the letter, model **Z** in the air. Have students echo the stroke descriptions as they write **Z** in the air with you. Ask questions such as these:
How many loops are in **Z**? *(one)*
How does **Z** end? *(with an overcurve)*

EVALUATE

To help students evaluate their writing, ask questions such as these:
Does your overcurve cross at the baseline?
Are your strokes smooth and even?
Is your **Z** about the same width as the model? *(visual, auditory)*

CORRECTIVE STRATEGY

NOT

Practice writing the curve forward and slant strokes so they flow smoothly into the overcurve at the baseline.

Name

Write.

Zelda   Zsa Zsa   Zach

Zeke was born in
New Zealand.

Write a sentence about a girl named Zelda.

EVALUATE Circle your best Z. Circle your best word.
Copyright © Zaner-Bloser, Inc.   **PRACTICE MASTER 39**

PRACTICE MASTER 39

REFOCUS

Review the letters **U**, **Y**, and **Z** by writing them on the chalkboard as the students say the strokes with you. Ask questions such as these:

Which letters are joined to the letter that follows? *(all)*

Which letters have a descender? *(Y, Z)*

Which letter doesn't have a loop? *(U)*

Write these words on the chalkboard:

United Yvonne Zeke

Ask students to do each of the following:

• Write the girl's name three times. Circle the descender. *(Yvonne)*

• Write the boy's name twice. Trace over the uppercase letter. Use a crayon to trace the overcurve stroke that ends the letter. *(Zeke)*

• Write the word that completes the country's name: _____ States. Write the word three times. Trace the undercurve stroke that joins the uppercase letter to the letter that follows. *(United)*

COACHING HINT

Use a hole punch to cut openings in a large letter made of card stock, construction paper, or other heavy paper and have students use yarn to lace the letter. (kinesthetic, visual)

WRITE AWAY

Ask students to write a story about a family camping trip in Yosemite, Yellowstone, or Zion. Participate by describing a typical family camping trip in a national park.

Review

Write names of national parks.

Yosemite   *Zion*

Yellowstone

Circle your best uppercase letter.

Write these sentences.

Ursula went to Yosemite.

Zion is in Utah.

Circle your best word.

74

EVALUATE

To help students evaluate their writing, ask questions such as these:

Which of your joinings are satisfactory?

Which of your joinings need improvement? (visual, auditory)

Circle V and *V* in these words.

Vultures fly high in the sky.
Vultures fly high in the sky.

Trace and write.

V is not joined to the letter that follows. Write words that begin with *V*.

Venus   Volga   Vittorio

Write a sentence that begins with *V*.

Vultures are large birds.

On Your Own Write a sentence that begins with *V*.

Circle your best *V*.

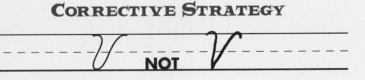

75

MODEL THE WRITING

Write **V** on guidelines as you say the stroke descriptions. To help students visualize the letter, model **V** in the air. Have students echo the stroke descriptions as they write **V** in the air with you. Ask questions such as these:

How does **V** begin? *(with a curve forward, slant)*
Where does **V** end? *(just below the headline)*

EVALUATE

To help students evaluate their writing, ask questions such as these:
Is your **V** about the same width as the model?
Are the curves in your **V** smooth and even?
Does your **V** end just below the headline? (visual, auditory)

CORRECTIVE STRATEGY

V **NOT** *V*

Make sure the undercurve is round.

Curve forward, slant
Undercurve
Overcurve

PRACTICE

Let students use laminated writing cards or slates to practice writing the letter.

WRITE AWAY

Ask students to think of a planet they want to know more about. Have them look up the planet in a children's encyclopedia and read the entry. Tell them to write about the planet and to illustrate their work. Participate by suggesting a planet you would like to know more about.

Name

Write.

Vermont Virginia

Valerie sat with her sister Violet.

Write a sentence that begins with *V*.

PRACTICE MASTER 40

Curve forward, slant,
   undercurve, (lift)
Slant

PRACTICE

Let students use laminated writing cards
or slates to practice writing the letter.

COACHING HINT

Write letters on pieces of poster board
or cardboard and laminate them.
Students can use them as a base to
form letters with clay. (kinesthetic,
visual)

Name

Write.

X X X X X X X

X X X X X X X

Xanthe Xavier Xena

*Xenia is a small
city in Ohio*

Write a sentence about a boy named Xavier.

EVALUATE Circle your best *X*. Circle your best word.
Copyright © Zaner-Bloser, Inc.   **PRACTICE MASTER 41**

PRACTICE MASTER 41

76

Circle *X* and *X*
in these words.

X-ray fish are as clear as glass.
X-ray fish are as clear as glass.

Trace and write.

X X   X X X X X X

X is not joined to the letter that follows. Write words that begin with *X*.

Xian   Xaviera   Xerxes

Write a sentence that begins with *X*.

X-ray fish are tiny.

On Your Own Write a sentence that begins with *X*.

Circle your
best *X*.

76

MODEL THE WRITING

Write **X** on guidelines as you say the stroke descriptions. To help
students visualize the letter, model **X** in the air. Have students echo the
stroke descriptions as they write **X** in the air with you. Ask questions
such as these:
How does **X** begin? *(with a curve forward)*
Where is the lift? *(after the undercurve)*

EVALUATE

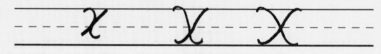

To help students evaluate their writing, ask questions such as these:
Does your **X** rest on the baseline?
Are your strokes smooth and even?
Is your **X** about the same width as the model? (visual, auditory)

CORRECTIVE STRATEGY

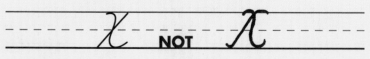

The second slant stroke crosses the first at the midline.

Walruses live on floating ice.

Walruses live on floating ice.

W W Trace and write.

W W W W W

W is not joined to the letter that follows. Write words that begin with *W*.

Wednesday   Wild West

Write a sentence that begins with *W*.

Walruses eat clams.

On Your Own Write a sentence about the Wild West.

Circle your best *W*.

77

Curve forward, slant
Undercurve, slant
Undercurve
Overcurve

PRACTICE
Let students use laminated writing cards or slates to practice writing the letter.

WRITE AWAY
Discuss with the students what happens on most Wednesdays. Ask them to write a description of a typical Wednesday.

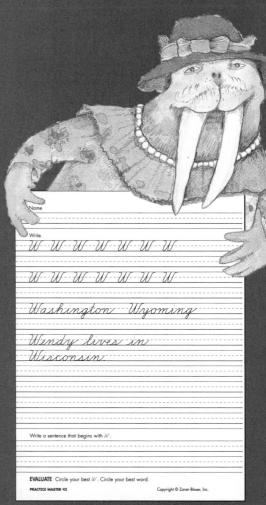

PRACTICE MASTER 42

MODEL THE WRITING
Write **W** on guidelines as you say the stroke descriptions. To help students visualize the letter, model **W** in the air. Have students echo the stroke descriptions as they write **W** in the air with you. Ask questions such as these:
Where does **W** begin? *(just below the headline)*
How many undercurves are in **W**? *(two)*

EVALUATE

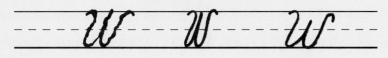

To help students evaluate their writing, ask questions such as these:
Are your strokes smooth and even?
Is your **W** about the same width as the model?
Does your **W** touch the headline three times? (visual, auditory)

CORRECTIVE STRATEGY

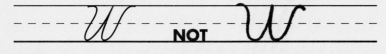

NOT

Say each stroke as you write the letter.

REFOCUS

Review the letters **V**, **X**, and **W** by asking questions such as these:

Which letters are joined to the letter that follows? *(none)*

Which letters begin with a curve forward? *(all)*

Which letters end with an overcurve? *(V, W)*

Write the following on the chalkboard:

      Ms. Voss
      Mrs. Xavier
      Mr. White

Review the use of titles with names. Remind students that a period is needed after each title. Ask volunteers to come to the chalkboard and write the titles and names of teachers or other people they know that begin with **V**, **X**, and **W**.

COACHING HINT: LEFT-HANDED WRITERS

Have the students hold their pencils farther back from the point than right-handed writers do. (kinesthetic)

WRITE AWAY

Ask students to choose a city named on page 78. Have them write two questions about that city, starting each question with the word *Where* or *What*. Participate by asking your own Where and What questions about a city of your choice.

Review

Write names of cities.

Vancouver   Xenia   Wuhan

Venice   Warsaw

Circle your best uppercase letter.

Write these sentences.

Xiao is from Xiang.

Circle your best word.

We read about Vienna.

78

EVALUATE

To help students evaluate their writing, ask questions such as these:

Which of your letters are shaped correctly?

Which of your letters need improvement in their shape?

Which of your letters are the correct size?

Which of your letters need improvement in their size? (visual, auditory)

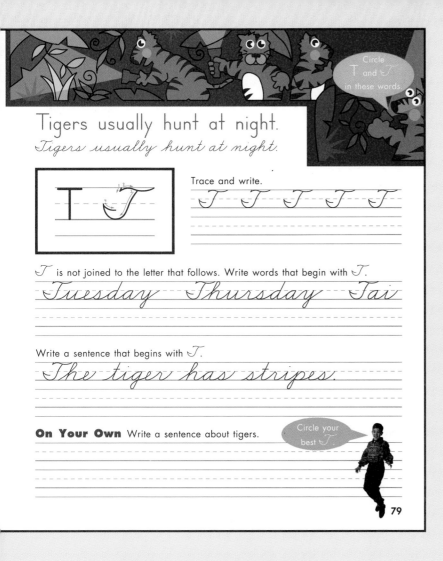

Tigers usually hunt at night.

Tigers usually hunt at night.

Trace and write.

T T T T T

T is not joined to the letter that follows. Write words that begin with *T*.

Tuesday   Thursday   Tai

Write a sentence that begins with *T*.

The tiger has stripes.

On Your Own Write a sentence about tigers.

Circle your best *T*.

79

Slant, curve forward
and right, (lift)
Doublecurve, curve up
Retrace, curve right

PRACTICE
Let students use laminated writing cards or slates to practice writing the letter.

WRITE AWAY
Ask students to write and illustrate a story that takes place on Thanksgiving. Participate by telling your own story about Thanksgiving.

Name

Write.

T T T T T T T T

T T T T T T T

Texas   Thanksgiving

Tyler and Taft were presidents.

Write a sentence about Thanksgiving.

EVALUATE Circle your best *T*. Circle your best word.

Copyright © Zaner-Bloser, Inc.   **PRACTICE MASTER 43**

PRACTICE MASTER 43

MODEL THE WRITING
Write **T** on guidelines as you say the stroke descriptions. To help students visualize the letter, model **T** in the air. Have students echo the stroke descriptions as they write **T** in the air with you. Ask questions such as these:
Where does **T** begin? *(at the headline)*
What is the first stroke in **T**? *(slant)*
Where does **T** end? *(below the midline)*

EVALUATE

To help students evaluate their writing, ask questions such as these:
Is your **T** about the same width as the model?
Does your **T** begin at the headline?
Does your last stroke curve right? (visual, auditory)

CORRECTIVE STRATEGY

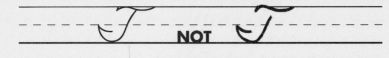

T **NOT** *T*

Do not leave space between the top and the body.

Slant, curve forward
and right, (lift)
Doublecurve, curve up
Retrace, curve right,
(lift)
Slide right

PRACTICE

Let students use laminated writing cards
or slates to practice writing the letter.

COACHING HINT

Students who hold the pencil too tightly
or do not use the correct position may
benefit from the use of the Zaner-
Bloser Writing Frame. This teaching aid
adapts for either right-hand or left-hand
use and fosters correct hand position
and arm movement.

Name

Write.

F F F F F F

F F F F F F

Fawn Florida French

France is a large
country in Europe

Write a sentence about the state of Florida.

EVALUATE Circle your best F. Circle your best word.
PRACTICE MASTER 44   Copyright © Zaner-Bloser, Inc.

PRACTICE MASTER 44

Circle F and F
in these words.

Flamingos have webbed feet.
Flamingos have webbed feet.

Trace and write.

F F F F F

F is not joined to the letter that follows. Write words that begin with F.

February Friday Faye

Write a sentence that begins with F.

Flamingos eat shellfish.

On Your Own Write a sentence about flamingos.

Circle your
best F.

MODEL THE WRITING

Write **F** on guidelines as you say the stroke descriptions. To help
students visualize the letter, model **F** in the air. Have students echo the
stroke descriptions as they write **F** in the air with you. Ask questions
such as these:
How are **T** and **F** alike? (There is a T in F.)
How are they different? (In **F**, the last stroke is a slide right.)

EVALUATE

To help students evaluate their writing, ask questions such as these:
Does your **F** rest on the baseline?
Is your **F** about the same width as the model?
Is your slide right stroke at the midline? (visual, auditory)

CORRECTIVE STRATEGY

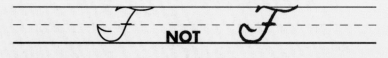

NOT

Pause before the retrace.

Circle I and *I* in these words.

Iguanas drop from trees into water.

Iguanas drop from trees into water.

Trace and write.

I I I I I I

I is not joined to the letter that follows. Write words that begin with *I*.

Indiana Illinois Idaho

Write a sentence that begins with *I*.

Iguanas are big lizards.

On Your Own Write a sentence that begins with *I*.

Circle your best *I*.

81

Overcurve
Curve down and up
Retrace, curve right

PRACTICE
Let students use laminated writing cards or slates to practice writing the letter.

WRITE AWAY
Ask students to write the first paragraph of their autobiographies. Participate by telling a story about yourself.

MODEL THE WRITING

Write **I** on guidelines as you say the stroke descriptions. To help students visualize the letter, model **I** in the air. Have students echo the stroke descriptions as they write **I** in the air with you. Ask questions such as these:

Where does **I** begin? *(just below the baseline)*

Where is the pause in **I**? *(at the midline before the retrace)*

EVALUATE

To help students evaluate their writing, ask questions such as these:

Does your **I** begin just below the baseline?

Is the slant of your **I** correct?

Is your **I** about the same size as the model? (visual, auditory)

CORRECTIVE STRATEGY

I **NOT** *I*

Pause after the curve at the midline and retrace.

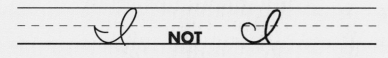

PRACTICE MASTER 45

**Overcurve
Slant
Loop back, overcurve**

PRACTICE
Let students use laminated writing cards or slates to practice writing the letter.

COACHING HINT
Have students use a pencil with #2 or softer lead. Make sure they do not apply a lot of pressure to their pencil as they write.

PRACTICE MASTER 46

82

Circle J and *J* in these words.

Jaguars have many spots.
Jaguars have many spots.

J *J*	Trace and write.
	J J J J J J J

J is joined to the letter that follows. Write words that begin with *J*.

January   June   July

Write a sentence that begins with *J*.

Jaguars live in jungles.

On Your Own Write a sentence about January, June, or July.

Circle your best *J*

82

MODEL THE WRITING
Write **J** on guidelines as you say the stroke descriptions. To help students visualize the letter, model **J** in the air. Have students echo the stroke descriptions as they write **J** in the air with you. Ask questions such as these:
Where does **J** begin? *(just below the baseline)*
Where do the two loops close? *(at the baseline)*
How does **J** begin? *(with an overcurve)*
How does **J** end? *(with an overcurve)*

EVALUATE

J   J

To help students evaluate their writing, ask questions such as these:
Does your **J** begin just below the baseline?
Do your loops close at the baseline? *(visual, auditory)*

CORRECTIVE STRATEGY

J   **NOT**   *J*

Make sure the descender fills the space.

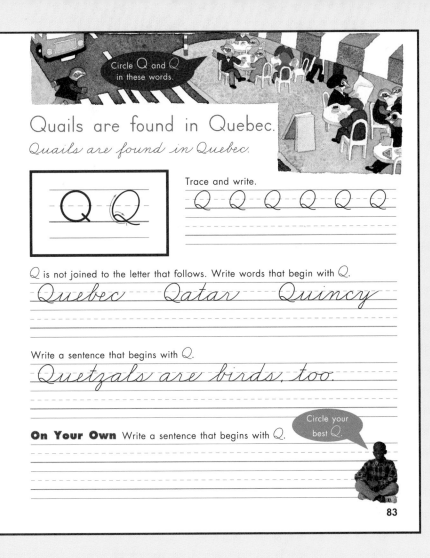

Circle Q and Q in these words.

Quails are found in Quebec.
Quails are found in Quebec.

Trace and write.

Q Q Q Q Q Q

Q is not joined to the letter that follows. Write words that begin with Q.

Quebec   Qatar   Quincy

Write a sentence that begins with Q.

Quetzals are birds, too.

On Your Own Write a sentence that begins with Q.

Circle your best Q

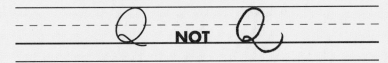

83

Q

Curve back, overcurve
Curve down, retrace
Curve forward, curve
under

PRACTICE
Let students use laminated writing cards or slates to practice writing the letter.

WRITE AWAY
Ask students to write a silly poem about quails and their tails. Participate by making up a silly poem of your own.

MODEL THE WRITING
Write **Q** on guidelines as you say the stroke descriptions. To help students visualize the letter, model **Q** in the air. Have students echo the stroke descriptions as they write **Q** in the air with you. Ask questions such as these:
Where does **Q** begin? *(at the baseline)*
Where does **Q** end? *(just below the baseline)*

EVALUATE

Q   Q   Q

To help students evaluate their writing, ask questions such as these:
Does your **Q** begin at the baseline?
Is your **Q** about the same width as the model?
Is your **Q** closed? (visual, auditory)

CORRECTIVE STRATEGY

Q   NOT   Q

The curve under stroke ends below the baseline.

Name

Write.

Q Q Q Q Q Q Q
Q Q Q Q Q Q Q
Quebec   Qatar   Quinn
Quentin is from
Queens, New York

Write a sentence that begins with the word *Quietly*.

EVALUATE Circle your best Q. Circle your best word.
Copyright © Zaner-Bloser, Inc.   PRACTICE MASTER 47

PRACTICE MASTER 47

83

Review the letters **T, F, I, J,** and **Q** by writing them on the chalkboard as the students say the strokes with you. Ask questions such as these:

Which letter is joined to the letter that follows? *(J)*

Which letters are not joined to the letter that follows? *(T, F, I, Q)*

Which letters begin at the headline? *(T, F)*

Which letters begin below the baseline? *(I, J)*

Which letter ends below the baseline? *(Q)*

Ask five volunteers to come to the chalkboard. Have them write one of the following uppercase letters: **T, F, I, J, Q.** Have each volunteer demonstrate the formation of the letter, then answer the following questions:

- Where does your letter begin?
- Where does your letter end?
- Does your letter have a descender?
- Does your letter join to the letter that follows?

COACHING HINT

Tell students they can increase their handwriting speed by eliminating excessive loops and flourishes from their writing. (visual)

WRITE AWAY

Ask students to choose one of the countries named on page 84 and to write a sentence explaining why they would like to go there. Participate by telling which country you would like to visit and why.

84

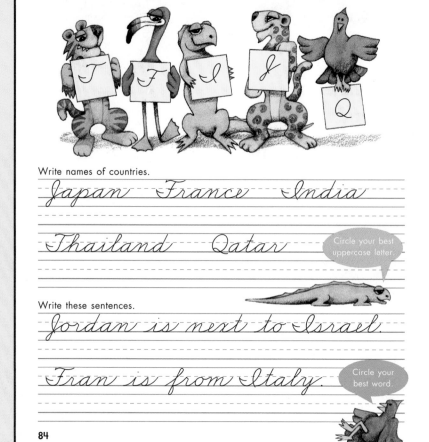

Review

Write names of countries.

Japan   France   India

Thailand   Qatar

Circle your best uppercase letter.

Write these sentences.

Jordan is next to Israel.

Fran is from Italy.

Circle your best word.

84

EVALUATE

To help students evaluate their writing, ask questions such as these:

Which of your letters are satisfactory?

Which of your letters need improvement? (visual, auditory)

Manuscript Maintenance: Secret Code

The answer to each riddle is written in code. Write the correct letters using your best uppercase manuscript.

1	2	3	4	5	6	7	8	9	10	11	12	13
Z	A	Y	B	X	C	W	D	V	E	U	F	T

14	15	16	17	18	19	20	21	22	23	24	25	26
G	S	H	R	I	Q	J	P	K	O	L	N	M

What animal talks a lot? 3 2 22

YAK

You use this animal to play baseball. 4 2 13

BAT

What kind of animal has a key, but doesn't open a door? 8 23 25 22 10 3

DONKEY

What type of fish is the richest? 14 23 24 8 12 18 15 16

GOLDFISH

What bird is present at every meal? 15 7 2 24 24 23 7

SWALLOW

The alphabet goes from A to Z. What animal goes from Z to A? 1 10 4 17 2

ZEBRA

What do camels have that no other animals have? 4 2 4 3   6 2 26 10 24 15

BABY CAMELS

85

EVALUATE

To help students evaluate their writing, ask questions such as these:
Is your spacing between letters correct?
Is your spacing between words correct? (visual, auditory)

good spacing. Write

Show an example of correct spacing between letters, words, and sentences. Remind students that letters and words that are too close together or too far apart make writing difficult to read. Provide opportunities to practice good spacing of letters and words on the handwriting guidelines.

COACHING HINT

You may wish to have students do the following activities for reinforcement of manuscript writing.

1. Label pictures and objects.
2. Write the names of friends and pets.
3. Prepare invitations to parties.
4. List games for parties.
5. Send holiday greetings to parents and friends.
6. Write about excursions to centers of interest in the community. (visual)

WRITE AWAY

Ask students to design a pet food package, using their best manuscript to write the name and contents. Participate by having available empty dry pet food boxes or magazine ads of pet food products.

Undercurve, loop, curve
forward
Doublecurve, curve up
Retrace, curve right

PRACTICE

Let students use laminated writing cards or slates to practice writing the letter.

COACHING HINT

Slates are great for letter practice. After you have modeled a letter, ask students to write on their slates before they write in their books or on paper.

Name

Write.

G G G G G G G

G G G G G G G

Greece Gwen George

*Georgia is a southern
state*

Write a sentence that begins with *G*.

EVALUATE Circle your best *G*. Circle your best word.

PRACTICE MASTER 48   Copyright © Zaner-Bloser, Inc.

PRACTICE MASTER 48

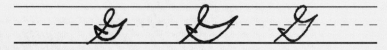

Circle *G* and *G* in these words.

Geese fly south for the winter.

Geese fly south for the winter.

SOUTH

Trace and write.

G *G*   *G G G G G*

G is not joined to the letter that follows. Write words that begin with *G*.

Georgia Grace Garth

Write a sentence that begins with *G*.

Gulls steal goose eggs.

On Your Own Write a sentence that begins with *G*.

Circle your best *G*.

86

MODEL THE WRITING

Write **G** on guidelines as you say the stroke descriptions. To help students visualize the letter, model **G** in the air. Have students echo the stroke descriptions as they write **G** in the air with you. Ask questions such as these:
Where does **G** begin? *(at the baseline)*
Where does the retrace begin? *(at the midline)*

EVALUATE

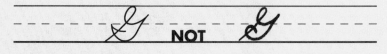

To help students evaluate their writing, ask questions such as these:
Is your loop written from midline to headline?
Is your **G** about the same width as the model?
Does your curve right stroke touch the midline and extend through the undercurve? (visual, auditory)

CORRECTIVE STRATEGY

G   NOT   *G*

Pause before the retrace.

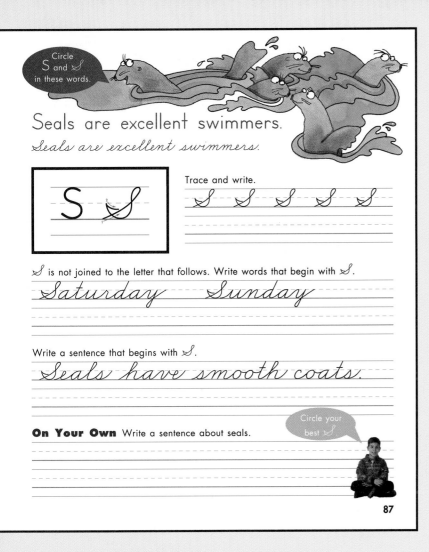

Circle **S** and 𝒮 in these words.

Seals are excellent swimmers.
Seals are excellent swimmers.

Trace and write.

𝒮 is not joined to the letter that follows. Write words that begin with 𝒮.

Saturday   Sunday

Write a sentence that begins with 𝒮.

Seals have smooth coats.

On Your Own Write a sentence about seals.

Circle your best 𝒮

MODEL THE WRITING

Write **S** on guidelines as you say the stroke descriptions. To help students visualize the letter, model **S** in the air. Have students echo the stroke descriptions as they write **S** in the air with you. Ask questions such as these:
Where does **S** begin? *(at the baseline)*
How many undercurves are in **S**? *(one)*
How many loops are in **S**? *(one)*

EVALUATE

To help students evaluate their writing, ask questions such as these:
Does your **S** have correct slant?
Is your retrace, curve right formed correctly?
Does your curve right stop before the undercurve?

CORRECTIVE STRATEGY

NOT

Close the loop at the midline.

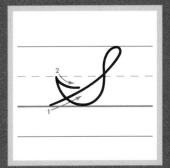

Undercurve, loop
Curve down and up
Retrace, curve right

PRACTICE
Let students use laminated writing cards or slates to practice writing the letter.

WRITE AWAY
Ask students to write a journal entry describing their activities last Saturday or Sunday. Participate by describing something you did last weekend.

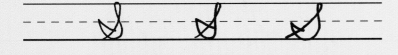

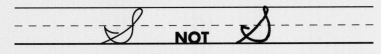

PRACTICE MASTER 49

**Undercurve
Loop, curve down
Loop, curve under**

PRACTICE

Let students use laminated writing cards or slates to practice writing the letter.

COACHING HINT

As students near the completion of their handwriting texts, make them aware of their improvement. Comparing students' writing with samples from the beginning of the year provides motivation for further progress, particularly for students who have had difficulties with handwriting. (visual)

Name _____

Write.

L L L L L L L

L L L L L L L

Lancelot London Lucy

Loch Ness is a lake
in Scotland.

Write a sentence that begins with the word Let's.

EVALUATE Circle your best L. Circle your best word.
PRACTICE MASTER 50   Copyright © Zaner-Bloser, Inc.

PRACTICE MASTER 50

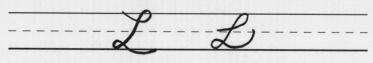

Llamas are related to camels.

Llamas are related to camels.

Trace and write.

L L   L L L L

L is not joined to the letter that follows. Write words that begin with L.

London   Little League

Write a sentence that begins with L.

Llamas have long necks.

On Your Own Write a sentence that begins with L. *Circle your best L*

MODEL THE WRITING

Write **L** on guidelines as you say the stroke descriptions. To help students visualize the letter, model **L** in the air. Have students echo the stroke descriptions as they write **L** in the air with you. Ask questions such as these:

How many loops are in **L**? *(two)*
Where does **L** begin? *(at the midline)*
Where does **L** end? *(just below the baseline)*

EVALUATE

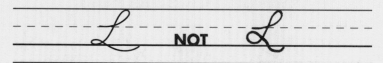

To help students evaluate their writing, ask questions such as these:
Does your **L** begin at the midline?
Does your **L** end just below the baseline? (visual, auditory)

CORRECTIVE STRATEGY

L   NOT   L

The lower loop is horizontal and rests on the baseline.

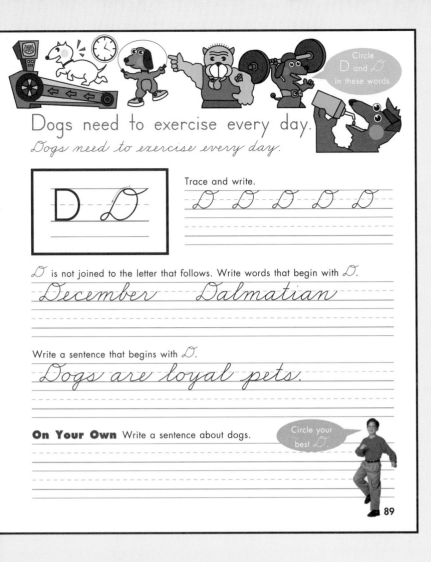

Dogs need to exercise every day.

Dogs need to exercise every day.

Circle D and *D* in these words.

Trace and write.

$\mathcal{D}$ $\mathcal{D}$ $\mathcal{D}$ $\mathcal{D}$ $\mathcal{D}$ $\mathcal{D}$

$\mathcal{D}$ is not joined to the letter that follows. Write words that begin with $\mathcal{D}$.

December   Dalmatian

Write a sentence that begins with $\mathcal{D}$.

Dogs are loyal pets.

On Your Own Write a sentence about dogs.

Circle your best *D*

89

MODEL THE WRITING

Write **D** on guidelines as you say the stroke descriptions. Model **D** in the air. Have students echo the stroke descriptions as they write **D** in the air with you. Ask questions such as these:

How many loops are in **D**? *(two)*
How many times does **D** touch the baseline? *(two)*
Where does **D** begin? *(at the headline)*

EVALUATE

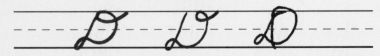

To help students evaluate their writing, ask questions such as these:
Does your **D** touch the baseline two times?
Is your **D** closed?
Does your **D** end at the headline? (visual, auditory)

CORRECTIVE STRATEGY

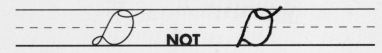
NOT

Practice the doublecurve stroke that begins **D** and then "rest" the loop on the baseline.

Doublecurve
Loop, curve down and
up
Loop, curve right

PRACTICE

Let students use laminated writing cards or slates to practice writing the letter.

WRITE AWAY

Ask students to write and illustrate a story with the title "My Life as a Dog." Participate by naming a kind of dog you would like to be and describing a typical day.

Name

Write.

$\mathcal{D}$ $\mathcal{D}$ $\mathcal{D}$ $\mathcal{D}$ $\mathcal{D}$ $\mathcal{D}$ $\mathcal{D}$

$\mathcal{D}$ $\mathcal{D}$ $\mathcal{D}$ $\mathcal{D}$ $\mathcal{D}$ $\mathcal{D}$ $\mathcal{D}$

Dennis   Drew   Doug

Debbie moved to Dover,
Delaware.

Write a sentence that begins with $\mathcal{D}$.

EVALUATE Circle your best $\mathcal{D}$. Circle your best word.
Copyright © Zaner-Bloser, Inc.   **PRACTICE MASTER 51**

PRACTICE MASTER 51

Write the letters **G**, **S**, **L**, and **D** on the chalkboard. Ask students to name the strokes as you form the letters. Ask questions such as these:

Which letters are joined to the letter that follows? *(none)*

Which letters begin with an under-curve? *(G, S, L)*

Which letter does not end with a curve right? *(L)*

Write the following names on the chalkboard in manuscript. Have students write each name twice in cursive.

Dave Lewis
Gail Sanders
Sari Dennis
Leandro Gamon

COACHING HINT

The folded-paper technique provides a quick check of letter formation. After students have written the letter three times on practice paper, have them fold the paper back and under, just above the letters written. By placing the paper directly below the model in the book, the letters that have been written may easily be compared with the model to determine likenesses and differences. (kinesthetic, visual)

WRITE AWAY

Ask students to write and illustrate a story entitled "A Day in the Desert." Participate by telling your own story about a day spent in the desert.

90

Review

Write names of deserts.

Death Valley   Gibson

Sahara   Libyan

Circle your best uppercase letter.

Write these sentences.

Sol saw the Great Sandy.

Li saw the Gobi.

Circle your best word.

90

EVALUATE

To help students evaluate their writing, ask questions such as these:
Which of your letters are satisfactory?
Which of your letters need improvement? (visual, auditory)

Circle P and P in these words.

Porcupines have many sharp quills.

Porcupines have many sharp quills.

Trace and write.

P   P   P   P   P

P is not joined to the letter that follows. Write words that begin with P.

Pluto Paris Pierre Pru

Write a sentence that begins with P.

Porcupines are rodents.

On Your Own Write a sentence about porcupines.

Circle your best P

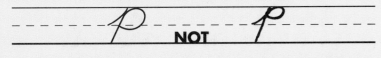

91

Undercurve, slant
Retrace, curve forward
and back

PRACTICE
Let students use laminated writing cards or slates to practice writing the letter.

WRITE AWAY
Ask students to write tongue twisters using the letters **P** and **p**. Have them trade their tongue twisters. Challenge students to read them aloud quickly three times. Participate by making up a tongue twister using the letters **P** and **p**. (visual, auditory)

MODEL THE WRITING
Write **P** on guidelines as you say the stroke descriptions. Model **P** in the air. Have students echo the stroke descriptions as they write **P** in the air with you. Ask questions such as these:
Where does **P** begin? *(at the midline)*
How does **P** begin? *(with an undercurve)*
Where is the retrace? *(at the bottom of the slant stroke)*

EVALUATE

P   P   P

To help students evaluate their writing, ask questions such as these:
Does your **P** begin at the midline?
Is your **P** about the same width as the model?
Is your **P** closed? (visual, auditory)

CORRECTIVE STRATEGY

P   **NOT**   P

The forward oval curves around and goes below the midline.

Name

Write.

P P P P P P P

P P P P P P P

Peter Pan   Pied Piper

*Patty lives in
Pittsburgh*

Write a sentence about Peter Pan.

EVALUATE Circle your best P. Circle your best word.
PRACTICE MASTER 52   Copyright © Zaner-Bloser, Inc.

PRACTICE MASTER 52

91

Undercurve, slant
Retrace, curve forward
    and back
Curve forward,
    undercurve

PRACTICE

Let students use laminated writing cards or slates to practice writing the letter.

COACHING HINT

Give each student a card on which one of the basic strokes is written. Tell the students to write that basic stroke on paper and to write all the uppercase and lowercase letters that have that basic stroke. (kinesthetic, visual)

Rhinos use mud to block the sun.

Rhinos use mud to block the sun.

Circle R and R in these words.

Trace and write.

R R R R R R

R is joined to the letter that follows. Write words that begin with R.

Rome   Rhine River   Ray

Write a sentence that begins with R.

Rain keeps rhinos cool.

On Your Own Write a sentence that begins with R.

Circle your best R.

92

MODEL THE WRITING

Write **R** on guidelines as you say the stroke descriptions. To help students visualize the letter, model **R** in the air. Have students echo the stroke descriptions as they write **R** in the air with you. Ask questions such as these:
Where does **R** end? *(at the midline)*
What is the ending stroke? *(undercurve)*

EVALUATE

To help students evaluate their writing, ask questions such as these:
Does your **R** begin at the midline?
Does your **R** end at the midline?
Does your retrace look like a single line? (visual, auditory)

CORRECTIVE STRATEGY

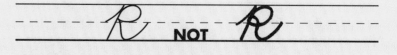

Pause at the slant stroke before beginning the second curve forward.

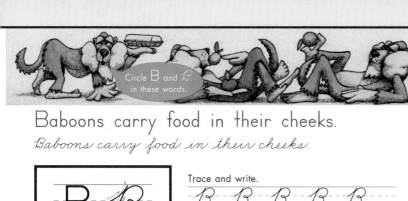

Circle B and *B* in these words.

Baboons carry food in their cheeks.

Baboons carry food in their cheeks.

Trace and write.

B   B   B   B   B

B is not joined to the letter that follows. Write words that begin with *B*.

Badlands   Beijing   Brett

Write a sentence that begins with *B*.

Baby baboons need care.

On Your Own Write a sentence about baboons.

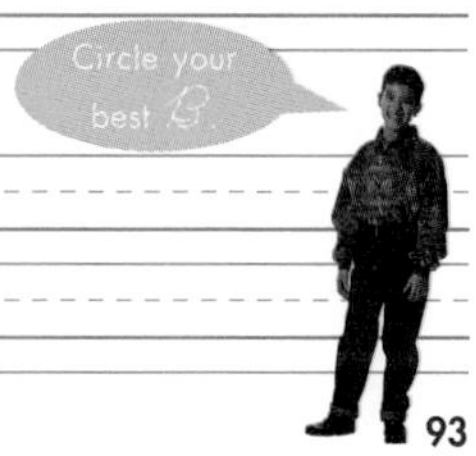

Circle your best *B*

Undercurve, slant
Retrace, curve forward,
  loop
Curve forward and
  back
Retrace, curve right

PRACTICE

Let students use laminated writing cards or slates to practice writing the letter.

WRITE AWAY

Ask students to write humorous titles and author names. Combine them to make a poster titled "Books We'd Like to Read." Participate by offering these examples: *All About Leopards* by I. C. Spotz; *Travel Tips* by Ima Lost and U. R. Tew; *Look to the Sky* by C. D. Birds.

MODEL THE WRITING

Write **B** on guidelines as you say the stroke descriptions. To help students visualize the letter, model **B** in the air. Have students echo the stroke descriptions as they write **B** in the air with you. Ask questions such as these:

How are **B** and **R** alike? *(They have the same beginning.)*
Where does the loop close? *(at the midline)*
What other letters have the curve right ending? *(I, G, T, F, and S)*

EVALUATE

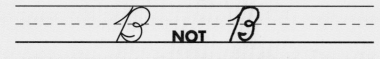

To help students evaluate their writing, ask questions such as these:
Does your **B** have correct slant?
Is your loop at the midline?
Does your **B** rest on the baseline? (visual, auditory)

CORRECTIVE STRATEGY

B **NOT** *B*

Make sure the ending stroke touches the slant stroke.

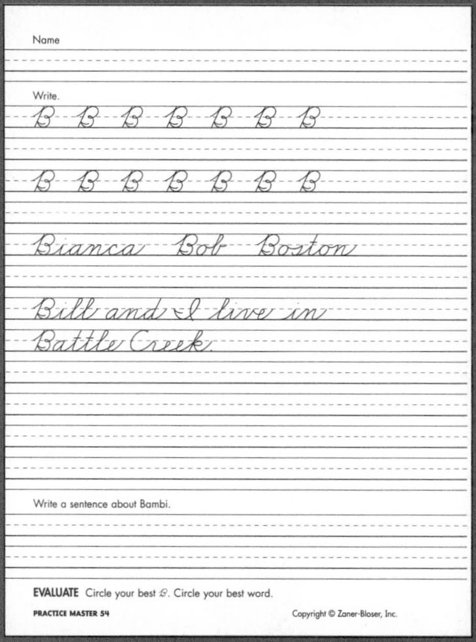

Name

Write.

B B B B B B B

B B B B B B B

Bianca   Bob   Boston

Bill and I live in Battle Creek.

Write a sentence about Bambi.

PRACTICE MASTER 54

REFOCUS

Write the letters **P, R,** and **B** on the chalkboard. Say the strokes as you write the letters. Ask questions such as these:

Which letter is joined to the letter that follows? *(R)*

Which letters are not joined to the letter that follows? *(P, B)*

Which letters are made with one forward oval? *(P, R)*

Which letter is made with two forward ovals? *(B)*

Ask a volunteer to face the chalkboard and form these letters in the air with broad, sweeping motions. Ask students to identify the letters.

COACHING HINT

Place a small amount of shaving cream on each student's desk. Direct students to spread the shaving cream over their desks. Ask them to practice the strokes and letters you call out. Repeat several times and allow time for students to experiment with various patterns of strokes. This is an effective exercise for reinforcing stroke and letter formations and also a good way to clean the desks. (kinesthetic)

WRITE AWAY

Provide students with a map of the United States. Have them write two state capitals and the states in which they are located. Participate by naming one state capital and the state it is in.

Review

Write names of state capitals.

Phoenix   Raleigh

Richmond   Boise

Circle your best uppercase letter.

Write these sentences.

Ryan moved to Boston.

Please come to Pierre.

Circle your best word.

94

EVALUATE

To help students evaluate their writing, ask questions such as these:
Which of your letters are satisfactory?
Which of your letters need improvement? (visual, auditory)

California Sacramento

New York Albany

Review Uppercase Letters

Write these uppercase letters in cursive.

A E C O

K X M Y Z

V W N H U

T F Q I J

D G L S

B R P

JOINING ALERT

Remember! These letters are joined to the letter that follows.

R K H J U A
Y C M Z E N

These letters are not.

G F O S T X B
Q L D P I V W

Write these words in cursive.

Memorial Day

Grand Canyon

United Nations

Puerto Rico

Circle your best word.

95

Tell students they now have studied and written all of the uppercase cursive letterforms. Guide them in a review of these letters with the following activity.

1. The letters **A, C, E, N, M, K, H, U, Y, Z, J,** and **R** are _____ to the letter that follows. *(joined)*

2. The letters **O, V, X, W, T, F, I, Q, G, S, L, D, P,** and **B** are _____ to the letter that follows. *(not joined)*

3. All uppercase letters are _____ letters. *(tall)*

4. The uppercase letters with descenders are _____. *(J, Y, Z)*

Have students review and practice the basic cursive strokes.

COACHING HINT

Students who have mastered the skill of writing the uppercase and lowercase letters without models should be given writing activities that will challenge them and require thinking.

WRITE AWAY

Ask students to describe how learning to write has affected or influenced them. Describe any memories you may have about learning cursive writing.

EVALUATE

To help students evaluate their writing, ask questions such as these:
Which of your letters are satisfactory?
Which of your letters need improvement?
Which of your joinings are satisfactory?
Which of your joinings need improvement? (visual, auditory)

Certificates of Progress *should be awarded to those students who show notable handwriting progress and Certificates of Excellence to those who progress to the top levels of handwriting ability.*

I can write in cursive.

Keys to Legibility

You've learned to write lowercase and uppercase cursive letters. Now you're on your own. Write a sentence in cursive.

_____

_____

_____

_____

In the following pages, you will write more words and sentences in cursive. You will look again at the size and shape of your letters. You will also improve your slant and spacing to help make your writing easy to read.

96

UNIT SUMMARY

This page tells students about the content, organization, and focus of the unit. Then students are introduced to the third and fourth keys to legibility: slant and spacing. The lessons that follow have writing activities for students to apply what they've learned. Evaluations focus on the four keys to legibility: size and shape, slant, and spacing.

PREVIEW THE UNIT

Preview the unit with students, calling attention to these features:

- hints about forming legible letters, writing with uniform slant, and achieving correct spacing

- opportunities to evaluate letter size and shape, slant, letter spacing, and word spacing

- a writing activity for manuscript maintenance

- review lessons that feature self-evaluation

Keys to Legibility: Slant

Help make your writing easy to read. Pay attention to slant.

Cursive letters have a forward slant.

a A z Z

POSITION
PULL
SHIFT

Check your paper position.
Pull your downstrokes in the right direction.
Shift your paper as you write.

If you are left-handed . . .

pull toward your left elbow.

If you are right-handed . . .

pull toward your midsection.

Check the slant.

Draw lines through the slant strokes in the letters.

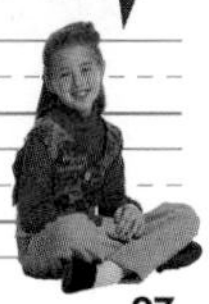

This is uneven slant.
This is good slant.

97

COACHING HINT: SLANT

Practicing slant lines at the chalkboard is a good way to improve poor slant strokes. Have students use soft, oversize chalk, holding it as they would hold a pencil. You may want to begin by placing sets of two dots about six inches apart and at the correct slant to mark the starting and stopping points of each slant stroke. (kinesthetic, visual)

correct slant

Tell students that in cursive writing all letters should have the same slant. Show an example of cursive writing with correct slant on the chalkboard. Use colored chalk to draw parallel lines through the slant strokes of the letters.

PRACTICE MASTERS FOR UNIT 4

KEYS TO LEGIBILITY: SPACING

Tell students that in cursive writing correct spacing is an important key to legible handwriting. There should be just enough space for a small oval between letters. Between words, the beginning stroke of one word should start near the ending stroke of the preceding word. A slanted line drawn from the end point of the last stroke to the baseline should touch both words. Show an example of cursive writing with correct spacing on the chalkboard. Use colored chalk to draw ovals and slanted lines.

Keys to Legibility: Spacing

Help make your writing easy to read.
Pay attention to letter and word spacing.

This better spacing is just right.
This word spacing is just right.

Is there space for *o* between letters?

spacing   spacing

Write the word correctly.

Is there space for \ between words?

Isthiseasytoread?
Is this easy to read?
Is this easytoread?

Write the sentence correctly.

COACHING HINT: SPACING

Remind students to shift their papers as they write to keep spacing consistent. (visual, kinesthetic)

 ## HANDWRITING AND THE WRITING PROCESS

Handwriting is an essential support skill for writing. When handwriting is fluent, legible, and automatic, students are free to concentrate on the content of their writing. Maintaining a consciousness about the importance of good handwriting will help students with every stage of the writing process.

Looking at Letter Size and Shape

Where can you find each animal? Write the name of the continent.

North America   Antarctica   Australia
Europe   Africa   South America   Asia

LEGIBLE LETTERS Remember! Tall letters touch the headline.
Short letters touch the midline.
Letters with descenders go below the baseline.

bison	North America
penguin	Antarctica
koala	Australia
llama	South America
Komodo dragon	Asia
hippopotamus	Africa
reindeer	Europe

Circle the name you wrote best.

99

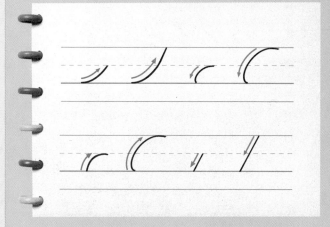

Review good formation of the four basic strokes. Ask volunteers to write examples of letters, both lowercase and uppercase, for each stroke.

Have students write their full names to see which stroke they use most often. Remind them that smooth, even strokes result in well-formed letters.

EVALUATE

To help students evaluate their writing, ask questions such as these:
Do your tall letters touch the headline?
Do your short letters touch the midline?
Do your letters with descenders extend below the baseline? (visual, auditory)

HANDWRITING AND THE WRITING PROCESS

Handwriting is important throughout the writing process. Students will have an easier time getting their thoughts in order when **prewriting** notes, lists, and webs are legible. Teachers will find it easier to understand writers' ideas, too.

To write with good size and shape, students should follow these guidelines:
Compare your letters to an alphabet chart in the classroom.
Make short letters half the height of tall letters.
Close the ovals in letters like **o** and **a**. Don't loop **i** and **t**.

COACHING HINT: LEFT-HANDED WRITERS

Have students tilt their papers to the right instead of to the left, as right-handed writers do.

WRITE AWAY

Ask students to write a paragraph telling which continent they would like to visit and why. Participate by telling why you would like to visit a particular continent.

LOOKING AT SLANT

asleep

Review correct slant of cursive writing. Write these words on the chalkboard: *toward, build, let's, trapeze, antelope.* Ask volunteers to use colored chalk to draw lines through the slant strokes.

Have students write the school name and use a crayon to draw lines through the slant strokes. Remind them to check the way they hold their pencils and place their papers.

COACHING HINT: LEFT-HANDED WRITERS

Have students review page 100 and check to see that their writing arm is in the proper position.

WRITE AWAY

Ask students to write the name of a make-believe language and the sound word for a dog barking in that language. Participate by making up a language name and a sound word for a dog barking.

Looking at Slant

What do you hear when a dog barks? Write the sound words in different languages.

POSITION
PULL
SHIFT
Remember! Check the way you hold your pencil and place your paper.

English	**Rrruf-ruf**
French	**Whou-whou**
German	**Vrow-vrow**
Japanese	**Won-won**
Russian	**Gruf-gruf**
Spanish	**Guau-guau**

Draw lines through the slant strokes.

Rrruf-ruf — **English**

Gruf-gruf — **Russian**

Won-won — **Japanese**

Whou-whou — **French**

Guau-guau — **Spanish**

Vrow-vrow — **German**

EVALUATE

To help students evaluate their writing, ask questions such as these:
Do your letters have satisfactory slant?
Which of your letters need better slant? (visual, auditory)

HANDWRITING AND THE WRITING PROCESS

Handwriting is important throughout the writing process. When students are **drafting,** encourage them to write legible, not "sloppy," rough drafts. As students develop a consciousness about legibility, their writing will be fluent and easy to read.

To write with good slant, students should follow these guidelines:
Always position your paper correctly on the desk.
Shift your paper as the writing progresses across the page.
Draw faint lines through your slant strokes to make sure all letters are slanting the same way.

Looking at Letter Spacing

Write the name of each group of animals.

a cloud of gnats   *a knot of toads*
a school of fish   *a bed of clams*

 LEGIBLE LETTERS   *This letter spacing is just right.*

  a bed of clams

  a school of fish

  a knot of toads

  a cloud of gnats

Is there space for *o* between letters?

On Your Own Make up a name for a group of skunks.

101

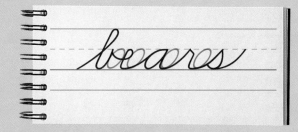

Review correct cursive letter spacing. Write the following animal names on the chalkboard: *giraffes, llamas, elephants, tigers, snakes.* Ask volunteers to use colored chalk to draw short ovals between the letters.

Have students write an animal name and use a felt-tip pen or colored pencil to draw ovals between the letters. Remind them that spacing will be correct if joinings are correct.

COACHING HINT: LEFT-HANDED WRITERS

Give left-handed students the opportunity to write at the chalkboard (where they will have greater freedom of arm movement) until they have learned correct letter formation.

WRITE AWAY

Ask students to write a description of one of the animal groups shown on page 101. Participate by describing an animal group of your choice.

EVALUATE

To help students evaluate their writing, ask questions such as these:
Is your letter spacing satisfactory?
Where does your letter spacing need improvement? (visual, auditory)

 ## HANDWRITING AND THE WRITING PROCESS

Handwriting is important throughout the writing process. Checking for legibility should always be a part of students' **revising** and **editing** routines. You and your students may wish to develop proofreading symbols to use for marking illegible sections of students' writing.

To write with good letter spacing, students should follow these guidelines:
Practice writing smooth joinings. Good joinings make good letter spacing.
Make sure there is room for an oval between letters.
Use hyphenation to avoid crowding or stretching letters at the end of a line.

Review correct cursive word spacing. Write the following animal phrase on the chalkboard: *a tiny gray mouse.* Ask a volunteer to use colored chalk to draw slanted lines between the words.

Have students write a four-word animal phrase and use a crayon to draw slanted lines between the words. Remind students that the beginning stroke of a word should start near the ending stroke of the preceding word (a little more space is needed before words that begin with the downcurve letters **a, c, d, g, o,** and **q**).

COACHING HINT: LEFT-HANDED WRITERS

Allow left-handed students to write at the chalkboard, where they can practice keeping their hands below the line of writing.

WRITE AWAY

Ask students to write a description of a funny book or movie. Participate by describing a funny book or movie of your choice.

Looking at Word Spacing

Laugh it up! Write the answer to each joke.

LEGIBLE LETTERS — *This word spacing is just right.*

What is gray and has four legs and a trunk?
a mouse on vacation

What is as big as an elephant but weighs nothing?
an elephant's shadow

How do you make an elephant float?
with ice cream and milk

What time is it when an elephant sits in your seat?
time to get a new seat

with ice cream and milk

a mouse on vacation

an elephant's shadow

time to get a new seat

Is there space for \ between words?

EVALUATE

To help students evaluate their writing, ask questions such as these:
Is your word spacing satisfactory?
Where does your word spacing need improvement? (visual, auditory)

HANDWRITING AND THE WRITING PROCESS

Handwriting is important throughout the writing process. Students should always use their best handwriting for **publishing** their work. Neat, legible writing shows courtesy to readers and makes a good first impression.

To write with good word spacing, students should follow these guidelines:
Make sure there is room for a slanted line between words.
Leave a little more space between sentences.
Move words to the next line in order to leave a margin on your paper.

YOUR PERSONAL BEST

I've Got a Dog

I've got a dog
  as thin as a rail,
He's got fleas
  all over his tail;
Every time his tail
  goes flop,
The fleas on the bottom
  all hop to the top.

Write this poem in your best cursive handwriting.
Pay attention to size and shape, slant, and spacing.

Circle your best line of writing.

103

EVALUATE

Have students use the self-evaluation process to evaluate their hand-writing. (visual)

FOCUS

Review with students the five-step self-evaluation process:

1. Question

Students should ask themselves questions such as these: "Is the slant of my letter correct?" "Does my letter rest on the baseline?"

2. Compare

Students should compare their handwriting to correct models.

3. Evaluate

Students should determine the strengths and weaknesses in their handwriting based on the keys to legibility.

4. Diagnose

Students should diagnose the cause of any difficulties. Possible causes include incorrect paper or pencil position, too much pencil pressure, and incorrect strokes.

5. Improve

Self-evaluation should include a means of improvement through additional instruction and continued practice. (auditory, visual, kinesthetic)

COACHING HINT: LEFT-HANDED WRITERS

The paper should be tilted so that the bottom right corner is a little to the right of the midsection. The downstrokes should be pulled toward the left elbow to obtain the correct slant.

WRITE AWAY

Ask students to write an original poem about a pet they have or would like to have. Participate by describing a pet you have or would like to have.

MANUSCRIPT MAINTENANCE: SMOOTHNESS

Review with students the proper way to hold a pencil. Remind students that writing that is too dark or too light is difficult to read. Emphasize that the amount of pressure used on the pencil determines the line quality.

too dark

pizza

too light

pizza

COACHING HINT

Errors in line quality may be a result of holding the pencil too tightly, using the fingers to draw the stroke, forming the stroke too quickly, varying the pressure on the pencil, or tilting the pencil at different angles. Be sure students are relaxed and are holding their pencils correctly and making strokes smoothly with one motion. Have students use arm and shoulder motion. Remind them not to draw the strokes. (kinesthetic)

WRITE AWAY

Ask students to use their best manuscript to write a "flier" from a pet-supply store. Participate by naming a local pet-supply store, telling a few of the products available (birdseed, dog food, cat toys), and stating the days and times the store is open.

Manuscript Maintenance: Word Math

Add and subtract words to make a new word.
Here is a sample to help you get started.

free + log - eel = frog

Write your answers in manuscript.

man + tops - ant =   mops

fowl + ox - owl =   fox

grape + sew - apes =   grew

grain + oat - rain =   goat

herb + earring - bear =   herring

On Your Own Write a word math problem of your own.

EVALUATE

To help students evaluate their writing, ask questions such as these:
Are any of your words too dark?
Are any of your words too light? (visual, auditory)

Looking at Letter Size and Shape

Write the name of a story in which you can find each animal.

Henny Penny

The Three Bears

Little Red Riding Hood

LEGIBLE LETTERS Remember! Tall letters touch the headline.
Short letters touch the midline.
Letters with descenders go below the baseline.

Who's been eating my porridge?

The Three Bears

The better to eat you with, my dear!

Little Red Riding Hood

The sky is falling!

Henny Penny

Circle the title you wrote best.

On Your Own Write the name of a favorite story.

105

Evaluate

To help students evaluate their writing, ask questions such as these:
Do your tall letters touch the headline?
Do your short letters touch the midline?
Do your letters with descenders extend below the baseline? (visual, auditory)

Handwriting and The Writing Process

You may wish to guide students through the writing process as they write a class retelling of a favorite story. For prewriting, ask volunteers to tell parts of the action out loud as you draw a story map or story diagram.

To write with good size and shape, students should follow these guidelines:
Compare your letters to the alphabet chart in the back of your book.
Make short letters half the height of tall letters.
Close the ovals in letters like **d** and **g**. Keep the loops open in **b** and **k**.

Looking at Letter Size and Shape

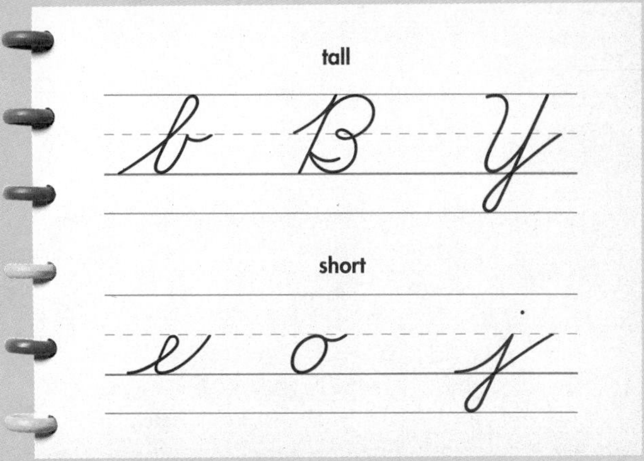
tall
short

Review the cursive size groupings. Ask volunteers to write examples of lowercase and uppercase letters for each grouping.

Have students write their full names to see which group they use more often. Remind students that tall letters touch the headline, short letters touch the midline, and some tall and short letters have descenders that extend below the baseline.

Coaching Hint: Left-Handed Writers

Students will benefit from the use of the Zaner-Bloser Writing Frame to foster correct hand position and arm movement.

Write Away

Ask students to write two sentences telling why a particular story is their favorite. Participate by naming a favorite story and your reasons for liking it.

green

Review correct slant of cursive writing. Write these words on the chalkboard: *heavy, laugh, wound, thousand, fifth.* Ask volunteers to use colored chalk to draw lines through the slant strokes.

Have students write their addresses and use a crayon to draw lines through the slant strokes. Remind them to check the way they hold their pencils and place their paper.

COACHING HINT: LEFT-HANDED WRITERS

Students can be grouped together for handwriting instruction at the chalkboard as well as at their desks.

WRITE AWAY

Provide resource materials such as children's encyclopedias. Ask students to write two unusual facts about animals. Participate by reading aloud an interesting animal fact of your choice.

Looking at Slant

Write the name of each animal champion.

POSITION PULL SHIFT Remember! Check the way you hold your pencil and place your paper.

Whale Shark

This bird is 8 feet tall and weighs 300 pounds.
Ostrich

This fish is 100 feet long and weighs 13 tons.
Whale Shark

This insect has a 10-inch wingspan.
Atlas Moth

Ostrich

This reptile is 16 feet long and weighs 1,150 pounds.
Saltwater Crocodile

Check your slant.

Draw lines through the slant strokes in the letters.

Atlas Moth

Saltwater Crocodile

106

EVALUATE

To help students evaluate their writing, ask questions such as these:
Do your letters have satisfactory slant?
Which of your letters need better slant? (visual, auditory)

HANDWRITING AND THE WRITING PROCESS

You may wish to guide students through the writing process as they write and illustrate a bulletin board of animal facts. Have students exchange drafts of their contributions with partners for help with revising and editing.

To write with good slant, students should follow these guidelines:
Always position your paper correctly on the desk.
Shift your paper as the writing progresses across the page.
Draw faint lines through your slant strokes to make sure all letters are slanting the same way.

Looking at Letter Spacing

An idiom is an expression that does not mean exactly what it says. Use animal idioms. Write each one next to its meaning.

barking up the wrong tree
letting the cat out of the bag

raining cats and dogs
in the doghouse

LEGIBLE LETTERS *This letter spacing is just right.*

telling a secret — letting the cat out of the bag

making a mistake — barking up the wrong tree

raining hard — raining cats and dogs

in trouble — In the doghouse

Is there space for ○ between letters?

107

EVALUATE

To help students evaluate their writing, ask questions such as these:
Is your letter spacing satisfactory?
Where does your letter spacing need improvement? (visual, auditory)

HANDWRITING AND THE WRITING PROCESS

You may wish to guide students through the writing process as they make illustrated books of animal idioms and other animal sayings such as "busy as a bee." As students revise and edit their books, remind them to check their handwriting, spelling, punctuation, and capitalization.

To write with good letter spacing, students should follow these guidelines:
Practice writing smooth joinings. Good joinings make good letter spacing.
Make sure there is room for an oval between letters.
Use hyphenation to avoid crowding or stretching letters at the end of a line.

Review correct cursive letter spacing. Write the following dog names on the chalkboard: *golden retriever, Saint Bernard, poodle, boxer, cocker spaniel.* Ask volunteers to use colored chalk to draw ovals between the letters.

Have students write the name of a type of dog and use a felt-tip pen or colored pencil to draw ovals between the letters. Remind them that spacing will be correct if joinings are correct.

COACHING HINT: LEFT-HANDED WRITERS

Encourage students to hold their hands and wrists correctly.

WRITE AWAY

Ask students to write a sentence using one of the animal idioms on page 107. Participate by using one of the idioms in your own sentence.

LOOKING AT WORD SPACING

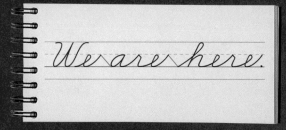

We are here.

Review correct cursive word spacing. Write the following fruit phrase on the chalkboard: *a big yellow banana.* Ask a volunteer to use colored chalk to draw slanted lines between the words.

Have students write a four-word fruit phrase and use a crayon to draw slanted lines between the words. Remind them that the beginning stroke of a word should start near the ending stroke of the preceding word (a little more space is needed before words that begin with the downcurve letters **a, c, d, g, o,** and **q**).

COACHING HINT: LEFT-HANDED WRITERS

Encourage students to practice their handwriting skills with other left-handed writers.

WRITE AWAY

Ask students to write a story that begins with one of the tongue twisters on page 108. Participate by using one of the tongue twisters as the first sentence of a story that you tell.

Looking at Word Spacing

Say each tongue twister three times as fast as you can. Then write it.

LEGIBLE LETTERS

This word spacing is just right.

Little lemmings like lots of lemons.

Monkeys mix millions of muffins.

Dalmatian digs dozens of daylilies.

On Your Own Write a tongue twister you know.

Is there space for \ between words?

EVALUATE

To help students evaluate their writing, ask questions such as these:
Is your word spacing satisfactory?
Where does your word spacing need improvement? (visual, auditory)

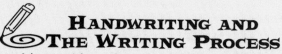

HANDWRITING AND THE WRITING PROCESS

You may wish to guide students through the writing process as they write tongue twister posters. Remind students to use their best handwriting on the published posters, which may be displayed in the school hallway or library along with a challenge, "Can You Say This?"

To write with good word spacing, students should follow these guidelines:
Make sure there is room for a slanted line between words.
Leave a little more space between sentences.
Move words to the next line in order to leave a margin on your paper.

If You Ever Meet a Whale

If you ever, ever,
  ever meet a whale,
You must never, never
  grab him by his tail.
If you ever, ever
  grab him by his tail—
You will never, never
  meet another whale.

Write this poem in your best cursive handwriting.
Pay attention to size and shape, slant, and spacing.

Circle your best
line of writing.

EVALUATE

Have students use the self-evaluation process to evaluate their hand-writing. (visual)

Certificates of Progress *should be awarded to those students who show notable handwriting progress and Certificates of Excellence to those who progress to the top levels of handwriting ability.*

FOCUS

Write the following sentence on the chalkboard in manuscript: *We will write a poem.* Ask four volunteers to write the sentence in cursive on the chalkboard, each showing one of the following:

- correct size and shape of letters
- correct slant
- correct spacing between letters and between words
- correct joining techniques

Encourage correct use of handwriting terms and stroke descriptions as the volunteers review these important elements of good handwriting.

COACHING HINT

Write a few words and sentences with several obvious errors on the chalkboard. Have volunteers come to the chalkboard to locate, identify, and correct the errors.

WRITE AWAY

Ask students to write a silly animal poem. Participate by reading aloud some poems from a variety of poetry books. The Shel Silverstein book *Where the Sidewalk Ends* is an excellent source of poetry well suited to this age.

POSTTEST

Remind students that at the beginning of the school year they wrote this poem as a pretest and evaluated their handwriting. As they write the poem in cursive as a posttest, remind them to use correct letter size and shape, uniform slant, and correct spacing. (visual, auditory, kinesthetic)

110

So Much

I have so much to say
And so much to write.
I want every word
To be written just right!

So Much
I have so much to say.
And so much to write.
I want every word
To be written just right!

Write the poem in your best cursive handwriting.

Circle your best line of writing.

110

EVALUATE

Have students use the keys to legibility to evaluate their handwriting. Suggest they compare this writing with their writing on the pretest, and discuss how their writing has changed. Meet individually with students to help them assess their progress. (visual, auditory)

Record of Student's Handwriting Skills

Cursive

	Needs Improvement	Shows Mastery		Needs Improvement	Shows Mastery
Sits correctly	☐	☐	Writes the undercurve to undercurve joining	☐	☐
Holds pencil correctly	☐	☐	Writes the undercurve to downcurve joining	☐	☐
Positions paper correctly	☐	☐	Writes the undercurve to overcurve joining	☐	☐
Writes undercurve strokes	☐	☐	Writes the overcurve to undercurve joining	☐	☐
Writes downcurve strokes	☐	☐	Writes the overcurve to downcurve joining	☐	☐
Writes overcurve strokes	☐	☐	Writes the overcurve to overcurve joining	☐	☐
Writes slant strokes	☐	☐	Writes the checkstroke to undercurve joining	☐	☐
Writes **i, t, u, w**	☐	☐	Writes the checkstroke to downcurve joining	☐	☐
Writes **r, s, p, j**	☐	☐	Writes the checkstroke to overcurve joining	☐	☐
Writes **a, c, d, q, g, o**	☐	☐	Writes with correct size and shape	☐	☐
Writes numerals **1-10**	☐	☐	Writes with correct slant	☐	☐
Writes **n, m, x, y, z, v**	☐	☐	Writes with correct spacing	☐	☐
Writes **e, l, h, k, f, b**	☐	☐	Regularly checks written work for legibility	☐	☐
Writes **A, C, E, O**	☐	☐			
Writes **N, M, K, H**	☐	☐			
Writes **U, Y, Z**	☐	☐			
Writes **V, X, W**	☐	☐			
Writes **T, F**	☐	☐			
Writes **I, J, Q**	☐	☐			
Writes **G, S, L, D**	☐	☐			
Writes **P, R, B**	☐	☐			

III

The Record of Student's Handwriting Skills is reproduced on Practice Master 56.

COACHING HINT
If a student needs improvement, reevaluate his or her writing following practice over a period of time. Invite the student to share in the evaluation.

EVALUATE

The Record of Student's Handwriting Skills serves to indicate each student's progress in mastering the skills presented. The chart lists the essential skills in the program. After the skills that are listed have been practiced and evaluated, you will be able to mark the Record of Student's Handwriting Skills for either *Shows Mastery* or *Needs Improvement.*

Shows Mastery Mastery of written letterforms is achieved when the student writes the letters using correct basic strokes. Compare the student's written letterforms with the letter models shown in the book. Keep in mind the keys to legibility (size and shape, slant, and spacing) when evaluating letters, numerals, punctuation marks, words, and sentences for mastery of skill. Observation will indicate whether a student has mastered such skills as pencil and paper positions.

Needs Improvement If a student has not mastered a skill, provide additional basic instruction and practice. First, determine the student's specific needs. Then, return to the initial teaching steps of the lesson for ways to help the student. To improve letterforms, have the student practice writing the letters in isolation and within words and sentences. Reinforce instruction through activities geared to the student's modality strengths. When mastery of skill is achieved, check *Shows Mastery.*

Index